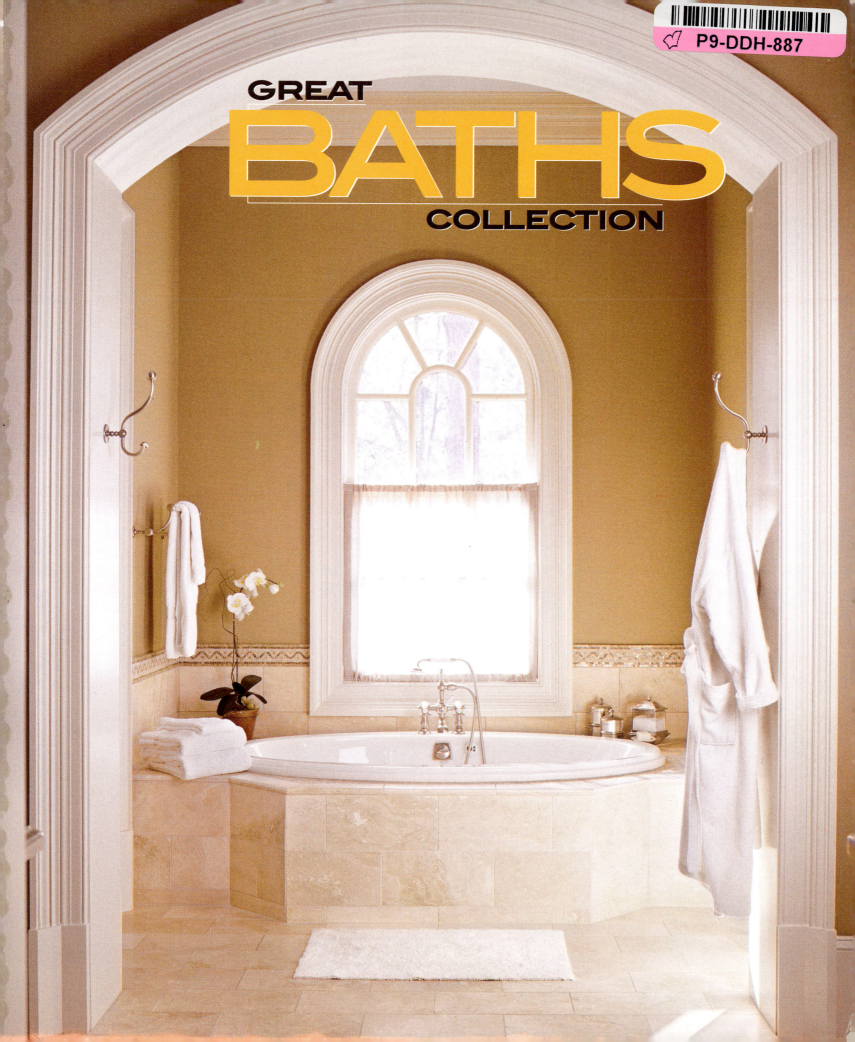

GREAT
BATHS
COLLECTION

Great Baths Collection
Editor: Paula Marshall
Project Manager/Writer: Catherine Staub, The Lexicon Group
Contributing Editors: Julie Collins, Dan Nelson, Kelly Roberson, The Lexicon Group
Graphic Designer: David Jordan
Copy Chief: Terri Fredrickson
Publishing Operations Manager: Karen Schirm
Senior Editor, Asset and Information Manager: Phillip Morgan
Edit and Design Production Coordinator: Mary Lee Gavin
Editorial Assistant: Kaye Chabot
Book Production Managers: Pam Kvitne, Marjorie J. Schenkelberg, Rick von Holdt, Mark Weaver
Contributing Copy Editor: Ira Lacher
Contributing Proofreaders: Sue Fetters, Beth Havey, Michelle Pettinger
Cover Photographer: Jeff McNamara
Indexer: Don Gulbrandsen

Meredith® Books
Executive Director, Editorial: Gregory H. Kayko
Executive Director, Design: Matt Strelecki
Executive Editor/Group Manager: Denise Caringer
Marketing Product Manager: Tyler Woods

Publisher and Editor in Chief: James D. Blume
Editorial Director: Linda Raglan Cunningham
Executive Director, New Business Development: Todd M. Davis
Executive Director, Sales: Ken Zagor
Director, Operations: George A. Susral
Director, Production: Douglas M. Johnston
Director, Marketing: Amy Nichols
Business Director: Jim Leonard

Vice President and General Manager: Douglas J. Guendel

Better Homes and Gardens® Magazine
Editor in Chief: Karol DeWulf Nickell
Deputy Editor, Home Design: Oma Blaise Ford

Meredith Publishing Group
President: Jack Griffin
Executive Vice President: Bob Mate

Meredith Corporation
Chairman and Chief Executive Officer: William T. Kerr
President and Chief Operating Officer: Stephen M. Lacy

In Memoriam: E.T. Meredith III (1933-2003)

All of us at Meredith® Books are dedicated to providing you with information and ideas to enhance your home. We welcome your comments and suggestions. Write to us at: Meredith Books, Home Decorating and Design Editorial Department, 1716 Locust St., Des Moines, IA 50309-3023.

If you would like to purchase any of our home decorating and design, cooking, crafts, gardening, or home improvement books, check wherever quality books are sold. Or visit us at: meredithbooks.com

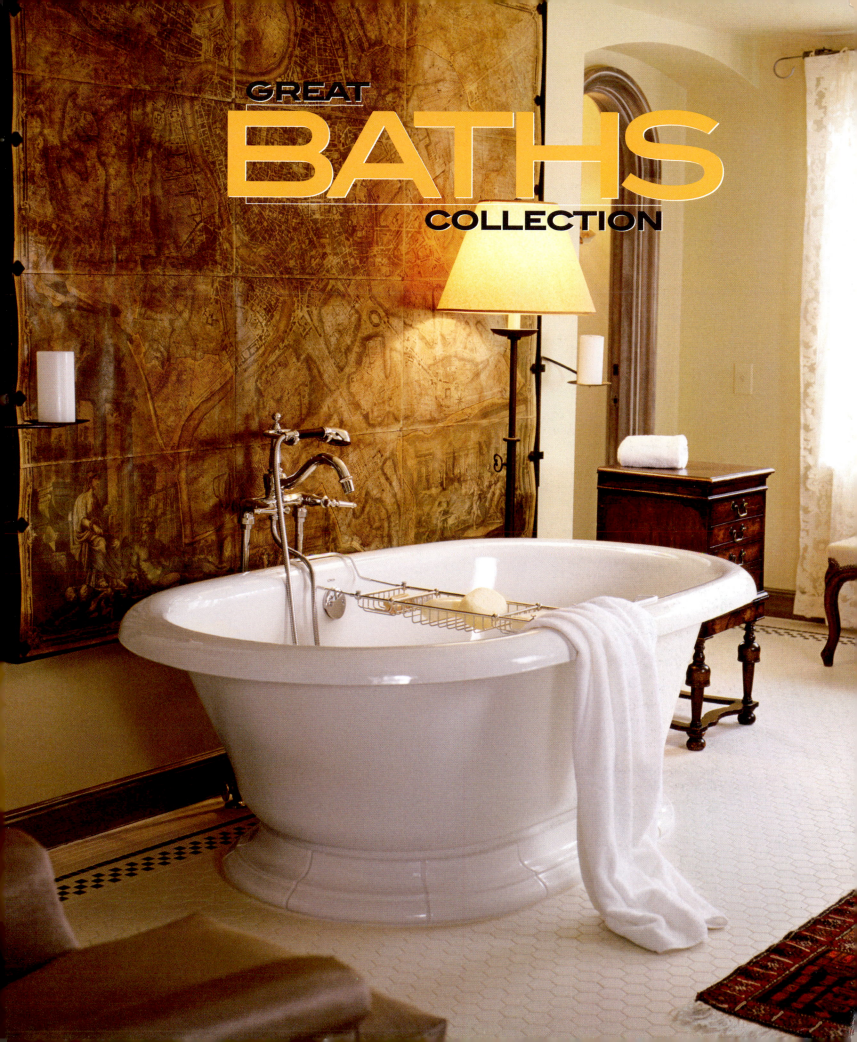

GREAT BATHS COLLECTION

GREAT BATHS COLLECTION

GREAT BATHS COLLECTION

1 BATHROOM TRENDS

You're guaranteed to find a few staples in almost every bath—the room wouldn't function without some combination of shower, tub, toilet, and sink. Yet technological advances, new textures, and color updates can transform an everyday bath into a haven of style and functionality. Whether you're updating a minimalist room or revamping a vintage bath, seek inspiration from these innovative products and styles. Replace the usual fixtures with high-tech toilets or sophisticated soaking tubs. Pair a vessel sink with fine furniture to create a vanity. Try replacing ho-hum wall coverings with the iridescent shimmer of glass tiles, natural texture of stone, or soft hues of ocean blue or mossy green. Don't forget personal touches to create the ideal retreat: Towel warmers and other pampering products ensure you'll never want to leave.

Toasty Towels

Step from the bath or shower and wrap yourself in a warm, fluffy towel. A staple in unheated Continental baths, towel warmers offer an easy way to capture spalike luxury in any bath. Metallic warmers complement bathroom fixtures, and funky shapes ensure these perches will never be mistaken for a plain old towel rack. Mount them on a wall or on the side of a vanity for easy access.

BASIN BEAUTY

VESSEL SINKS MAY NOT BE NEW, BUT THESE ABOVE-COUNTER BASINS' DISTINCTIVE STYLES GIVE THEM STAYING POWER. TODAY'S METAL, STONE, OR GLASS BOWLS PROVIDE A NEW TAKE ON THE OLD-FASHIONED; WASHBASIN; GRACE YOUR COUNTERTOP WITH A RUSTIC COPPER BOWL, SLEEK GLASS VESSEL, OR GLEAMING CHROME BASIN. THE VESSELS SIT ALMOST ENTIRELY ON TOP OF THE COUNTER AND ARE USUALLY PAIRED WITH TALL OR WALL-MOUNT FAUCETS. MAKE CERTAIN THE FAUCETS ARE LONG AND HIGH ENOUGH TO REACH THE BOWL, BUT NOT SO HIGH THAT WATER SPATTERS WHEN IT HITS THE BASIN. SEEK DURABILITY FOR HEAVY-USE BATHS—DELICATE BOWLS MIGHT NOT WITHSTAND THE DAILY ABUSE THAT SINKS ENDURE.

Vanity Fare

Bring elements of fine furniture into your bathroom to create a stylish, welcoming retreat. Antique dressers, hutches, and side-boards create functional, fashionable alternatives to the typical vanity. Freestanding furniture provides flexibility traditional bathroom cabinetry doesn't—should you tire of it, simply swap it for something else. Or create a signature piece for your bath by adding furniture-style doors, drawers, moldings, legs, or hardware to an existing vanity.

SIT IN THE LAP OF LUXURY AND SAVE SPACE WITH THE NEWEST IN LAVATORY INNOVATIONS. THIS PETITE WALL-MOUNT TOILET FUNCTIONS JUST AS WELL AS A FULL-SIZE, BUT THE DISAPPEARANCE OF THE TOILET TANK LEAVES MORE ROOM FOR STYLE. KEEP AN EYE OUT FOR THE NEW HATBOX VERSION TOO. THE STREAMLINED, TANKLESS TOILET IS POWERED BY AN ELECTRONIC PUMP ENCLOSED WITHIN THE BOWL, AND IT'S ERGONOMICALLY DESIGNED TO CONFORM TO THE BODY. THESE UNOBTRUSIVE VERSIONS CONSUME HALF THE SPACE OF THE TYPICAL TOILET AND ARE EASIER TO CLEAN. PLUS, YOU CHOOSE THE HEIGHT AT WHICH TO INSTALL THEM, A BOON FOR PEOPLE WANTING MORE LEGROOM OR WHEELCHAIR ACCESSIBILITY.

BETTER BATHS

SOAKING TUBS ARE REPLACING WHIRLPOOLS AS
SOPHISTICATED STAPLES IN MANY MASTER BATHS. TRY
THE ASIAN-INSPIRED VERSION SUNK INTO THE
GROUND, WHICH COMES IN MATERIALS SUCH AS
CEDAR, CERAMIC TILE, AND FIBERGLASS. AFTER
EMERGING FROM THE SHOWER, SLIP INTO THE DEEP
WELL FILLED WITH HOT WATER FOR A SOOTHING SOAK.
REPRODUCE THE CLASSIC CHARM OF A VINTAGE TUB
BY MAKING A SHAPELY FREESTANDING VESSEL THE
FOCAL POINT OF THE ROOM. SOME FREESTANDING
TUBS EVEN PULL DOUBLE DUTY, ALLOWING YOU TO
SINK INTO WATER UP TO YOUR CHIN WHILE OFFERING A
REVITALIZING MASSAGE. IF SOAKING IS A FREQUENT
PLEASURE, CONSIDER HAVING A TUB CUSTOM-MADE
TO FIT YOUR SHAPE AND BATHING PREFERENCES.

Capture the nostalgic aesthetic of subway tiles. These retro pieces are characterized by their shape—they're typically longer than they are high—and work for all-over style or combined with other tiles. Glossy white subway tiles on a wall make a room seem more spacious. Or jazz things up by pairing a strip of black with the white.

SHOWER POWER

You'll be singing in the shower with the newest batch of versatile, high-tech showerheads, designed to efficiently cleanse and rejuvenate. New fixed-position heads provide multiple sensations—such as a regular spray, narrow needle jet, and relaxing rain shower—all in one. Adjustable arm extensions, flexible necks, and handheld options enable water to hit directly where you want it; hydro-massage versions offer spa-worthy sprays. Instead of using a single wall-mount unit, combine multiple heads. Try a large, high spout with a handheld or sliding bar showerhead to ensure you're squeaky clean.

FLUID CURVES AND CLEAN LINES HIGHLIGHT THE FUTURISTIC FUNCTION OF TODAY'S MINIMALIST FAUCETS. SLEEK SINGLE-LEVER VARIETIES SAVE SPACE, WHILE SMOOTH WALL-MOUNT VERSIONS WITH LEVER HANDLES PAIR WELL WITH VESSEL SINKS. FAUCET FINISHES ARE LIMITLESS. BUT TRY POLISHED CHROME, BRUSHED NICKEL, OR STAINLESS STEEL TO HIGHLIGHT THE SIMPLISTIC SQUARE EDGES AND SMOOTH ARCS OF THESE FAUCET MASTERPIECES.

NATURAL CHARACTERS

FROM TEXTURED LIMESTONE TO SMOOTH PEBBLES, STONE MATERIALS ADD RUGGED SOPHISTICATION TO BATHS. IN TILE FORM, STONE PROVIDES PERMANENCE AND STRENGTH FOR FLOORING. FOR AN ALL-OVER RUSTIC FEEL, VARY THE TEXTURES, COLORS, AND SIZES OF THE TILES. SMOOTH PEBBLE FLOORING IN THE SHOWER OFFERS A MORE REFINED LOOK. TUMBLED MARBLE OFFERS THE ELEGANCE OF SMOOTH STONE WITH A LESS SLIPPERY TEXTURE. LIMESTONE PROVIDES ANOTHER EARTHY ALTERNATIVE: ALTHOUGH IT'S SOFTER THAN GRANITE OR MARBLE, LIMESTONE COMES IN A VARIETY OF FINISHES THAT ARE EASILY COMBINED. TO ADD MINIMAL STONE ELEMENTS TO YOUR BATH, TRY A GRANITE BOULDER SINK OR STONE KNOBS FOR VANITY DRAWERS.

THE GEMLIKE QUALITY OF GLASS TILES CAN BE
DECEIVING—THEY'RE NOT AS FRAGILE AS THEY LOOK.
USE THEM FOR FLOORS, WALLS, OR SHOWERS FOR A
SPLASH OF SHIMMERING COLOR. COVERING LARGE
PORTIONS OF A ROOM IN 1x1-INCH TILES GIVES THE
APPEARANCE OF LIQUID SPACIOUSNESS, OR USE A
MOSAIC OF IRIDESCENT COLORS FOR BURSTS OF
ENERGY IN A BATHING AREA.

HIP HUES

Don't miss the newest shades for baths, all of which combine high style with the tranquility of an at-home retreat. In small doses, ocean blue, mossy green, lime, lettuce green, or lavender do wonders for a countertop or shower curtain. Or go for all-over color in tiled showers or on painted walls. If you're not ready to commit to these colors long-term, turn to accessories such as towels, lotion bottles, and soaps for a quick change but palette-pleasing approach.

ESCAPE LIFE'S STRESSES WITHOUT LEAVING HOME BY TRANSFORMING YOUR BATH INTO A SPALIKE RETREAT. INDULGE IN AMENITIES DESIGNED TO MAKE YOU SIGH "AAH." CANDLES AND MUSIC PROVIDE AMBIENCE, AND TREAT YOURSELF TO A FRESH BOUQUET OF FLOWERS ON THE VANITY. KEEP BATHING NECESSITIES AND INDULGENCES, INCLUDING BODY SCRUBS AND SALTS, LOOFAHS, AND BATH OILS, WITHIN EASY REACH. INTRODUCE PAMPERING PRODUCTS INTO YOUR DECOR BY ARRANGING PRETTY SOAPS IN A DISH OR FILLING ANTIQUE GLASS BOTTLES WITH LOTIONS. WHEN EMERGING FROM THE SHOWER OR BATH, WRAP YOURSELF IN AN ENVELOPING, FLUFFY EGYPTIAN COTTON TOWEL BEFORE SLIPPING INTO PLUSH SLIPPERS AND A LUXURIOUS ROBE. FOR THE ULTIMATE RETREAT CONSIDER INSTALLING A GAS FIREPLACE, STEAM SHOWER, OR RADIANT HEAT UNDER THE FLOOR—ALL GUARANTEED TO KEEP YOU WARM AND RELAXED. OR SIMPLY CREATE THE PERFECT PERCH. A BENCH IN THE SHOWER OR A COMFORTABLE CHAIR IN THE BATHROOM OFFERS PLACES TO REST AT ANY POINT.

2 CONTINENTAL DESIGN INFLUENCE

Create an Old World retreat with a bath inspired by attention to fine details. Plastered walls, hand-glazed furniture treatments, and ornate moldings all contribute to the look of European-crafted baths. Incorporate or create architectural details such as classic arches to produce a formal, elegant atmosphere. Honed marble floors contrast with glossy ceramic wall tiles for additional elegance and style. Select ornate faucets with coordinating pulls for vanities. Or, to evoke softer Old World charm, utilize unmatched freestanding bureaus and hutches instead of built-in cabinets for a room that looks as if it were created slowly over time. If you have the space, install a fireplace for true continental luxury and warmth.

Chateau Nouveau

The luxurious and soothing tone of this master bath comes naturally. In its original state, the opulent French-inspired retreat was a bedroom and, despite its new purpose, the space retains a handsome level of welcoming comfort.

The transformation occurred when owners Fred and Sherrie Petermann began an ambitious remodeling of their 1875 Maryland manor. Combined with the antique character of their home, Sherrie desired an added dimension of European elegance.

"We wanted to create a bath that was restful and romantic and in keeping with the old-fashioned appeal of our home," says Sherrie, an interior designer. "We chose cabinetry, fixtures, and colors with those goals in mind."

Porcelain and brass faucets lend aristocratic sophistication to the marble countertop's subdued colors.

Evoking the casual relaxation of a chateau parlor, furniture and fine details such as the chaise longue, footrest, and fireplace set this room's tone.

To expand the visual space, a newly raised ceiling featuring deep crown molding creates a multilevel, vaulted effect. Adding an expansive, dramatic focal point, a broad mirror stretches from the mantel to the new ceiling, and a second, octagonal mirror is affixed to the larger mirror. "It made the fireplace smaller and more intimate," says Sherrie, "a perfect size for a bathroom."

Original to the room, the fireplace is reframed with nearly flawless marble. The golden unblemished stone extends to the counters, floor, and tub deck. "Marble floors and counters were often used in fine manor homes like this," Sherrie explains, "and I wanted to re-create that old-fashioned, elegant look here."

Building on the stately champagne-colored marble, the cabinetry is custom-made to exhibit refined furniture-like qualities. Brass faucets and drawer pulls add a polished, reflective element to the cream-toned cabinets. "I love French furniture and all of its fine detailing," Sherrie says, "so I decided to create a very French, very romantic room."

The alluring continental features evoke the feeling of an aristocratic parlor nestled in a modern bath. Almost white in tone, a pale, buttery color scheme imparts a soothing, richly luxurious mood. Providing a warm foundation, a patterned oriental rug balances the neutral color palette. Invitingly, a 1920s chaise longue occupies the center of the room, offering the promise of refined rest and relaxation.

For Sherrie the bath serves as a retreat for comfortable reflection. "It's the kind of bath you want to spend time in," she says. "You can sit and have a glass of wine before you go out for the evening."

THE VANITY ESTABLISHES A STATELY, ELEGANT AMBIENCE WITH MARBLE COUNTERS AND FURNITURE-LIKE DETAILS.

WITH A HINT OF PARISIAN DELICACY, SPARKLING FRENCH PERFUME BOTTLES ON THE VANITY BALANCE THE ROOM'S MUTED COLORS.

COUNTERING THE SUBDUED COLOR TONES, CURTAINS IN THE GLASS CABINET DOORS AND POLISHED BRASS DRAWER PULLS ADD BRIGHT ELEMENTS.

Continental Collage

In its original form this 1927 Spanish-style home in California offered plenty of Old World charm and sophistication. But a remodeling effort in the 1970s, featuring characterless white walls and fluorescent lighting, left the stately home feeling awkward and incomplete.

Hoping to build on the original architectural style, homeowners Ellen Bergeron and Gary Ottoson recognized this room as an opportunity to embrace their love of French and Italian styles. The result is a splendid fusion of Mediterranean elegance and singular artistic vision.

Designer Lori Erenberg, a former art and architectural history student, understood that the homeowners' vision relied on authentic details. Pushing out walls and combining old Mediterranean elements, Erenberg wanted to produce a serene reflection of Tuscan hillsides and the fields of Provence. "Everything should look natural, like it has an origin," Erenberg says, explaining her goal to find a pleasing balance.

The result is a bathing space that includes a soaking tub, an open shower, and a French window that opens onto a garden view. Recalling the designs of old European craftsmen, a new line of Italian tiles establishes the Old World tone on the walls and floor. "I used to go to Italy a lot when I was younger, to small towns on the Adriatic," Erenberg says. "This tile reminded me of the rooms in the homes there."

To complement the rustic bathing area, an ornate sink evokes the warm splendor of a Venetian villa. The sink is installed in a striking custom-made, antique-inspired cabinet. Burled wood veneer presents a distinctly 1920s French look, while marble contributes to the robust antiquated feel. Extending the stylistic references, Erenberg added a touch of Moroccan influence in the curving marble backsplash. The equally ornate sconces and ceiling

Seeking an authentic appearance, Italian tile provides the rustic look of Old World style.

Framed by elegant marble and evoking the serenity of a european villa, the bathing space features Italian tile and a garden view.

lamp provide a delicate touch of the California Revival style. "I didn't want anything too Italianate-heavy," Erenberg notes.

Natural light provides the final element: A new skylight and two windows create warmth and an aged, golden tone of romantic Europe. "It's not just decorating," Erenberg says, referring to the interplay of light, space, and classic details. "It's like making a collage."

The elegant confluence of rustic European-inspired styles more than pleases the homeowners. "I'm surrounded by Italian tile," Ellen enthuses. "I can listen to the birds singing and opera playing. I can smell the lavender water. It's absolutely spectacular!"

PRESENTING A GRAND, ROMANTIC EFFECT, THE VANITY FEATURES A BURLED WOOD VENEER AND A CURVING MARBLE BACKSPLASH.

ALONG WITH ITS RUSTIC TILE, THE SHOWER OFFERS MODERN AMENITIES SUCH AS A HANDHELD SPRAYER, STEAM, AND A BENCH.

A Whiff of Tuscany

Outside is a forest of redwoods, but from inside Veronica Napoles' master bathroom the view could be a grove of olive trees or the sea. "My goal was to not only make it more comfortable, but make it fit into what my long-term objective is with the house: to swing it into a more Mediterranean, warm feel—that Tuscan province feel," Veronica says.

Though the layout of the 11×10-foot room worked fine inside the 1916 California home, frosty, dark, sleek ultra-modern finishes clashed with Veronica's vision. Original locations of the fixtures remained intact, but all were restyled or replaced to fit with architect Fran Halperin's fresh design.

Veronica put her skills as an artist and designer to work in several spots, from vanity to tub. The vanity she designed sits 36 inches high rather than the standard 30 inches to eliminate stooping. Iron hardware accents the warm maple finish of the fir cabinets. The flush doors of the lower cabinets emphasize a smooth line, while a trio of sconces highlights a subtle vertical relief on the upper units. Topped with a mottled limestone counter, the vanity's drawers and doors provide a wealth of storage, and a sit-down cosmetic counter next to the sink allows for a

On her second try Veronica mastered the humidity requirements for the handmade concrete accent tiles. A weathered look and acid etching complement the Tuscan appearance.

Re-enameling turned the tub from gray to white. New faucets add sparkle. Limestone paves the tub's surround, and a display niche holds the perfect accent.

RE-ENAMELED WHIRLPOOL TUB
ACID-ETCHED CONCRETE TILES
ELEVATED VANITY HEIGHT
WINDOWS INSIDE SHOWER

practical grooming center.

Limestone also surfaces the floor, three walls of the shower, and the bathtub deck, its warm, neutral tone perfectly complementing the vaguely peach hue of the cabinets. A frameless glass door outlined with an arched entrance marks the shower opening. Windows inside the generous space wrap the view in redwood forest. That arch, marked with a keystone, is one of the room's unifying elements; it appears again in a display niche above the tub and the shape of the vanity's recessed mirrors.

Veronica kept the room's whirlpool tub; re-enameling transformed it from gray to white. Concrete tiles line the tub and vanity backsplashes. Veronica handcrafted them for a fraction of the retail cost. The peachy pigment and acid-etched weathered look of the molds—an ancient acanthus-leaf pattern and a 2-inch-tall bullnose edge—match the limestone tiles and the Tuscan look. Veronica

mastered the difficult curing and drying process on her second attempt, creating a uniform texture for the pieces.

The sleek finishes of the old room are just a memory, for the refreshed and restyled space brought Tuscany into the heart of Veronica's master bath.

AN ARCH MARKED WITH A KEYSTONE SIGNALS THE ENTRANCE TO THE SHOWER AND REPEATS ON A TUB DISPLAY NICHE AND IN THE VANITY'S RECESSED MIRRORS. WINDOWS FLOOD THE SHOWER WITH LIGHT AND A VIEW TO THE REDWOOD FOREST OUTSIDE.

SIZED AN EXTRA 6 INCHES HIGH, THE VANITY ACCOMMODATES VERONICA'S HEIGHT AND DOESN'T SHORT HER ON STORAGE. A SIT-DOWN COSMETIC COUNTER ADJOINS THE SINK.

A 1929 Italianate villa's romantic architectural heritage and spectacular views of the lush California countryside inspired interior designer Kathryne Dahlman when she remodeled the home's spacious master bath.

"My goal was to make as beautiful a bath as I could while staying true to the home's architecture," Dahlman says. The completed retreat combines natural sunshine and classic Italian style with breathtaking views of the San Rafael Hills and the Pacific Ocean.

Originally the long, narrow bath was chopped into compartments for the toilet, sauna, and shower. Dahlman's plan replaced the individual rooms with inviting openness, thanks to added square footage from an adjoining hall closet and arched openings which give the illusion of more space.

To offer maximum light and unhindered outdoor views while maintaining privacy, areas are separated with tiled arches and panes of glass instead of walls. A frameless glass enclosure surrounds the shower and an arched opening subtly separates the toilet from the tub area without obstructing natural light.

AN IDYLLIC VIEW BECAME THE BATHROOM'S NEW FOCUS. SOOTHING HUES, GLASS, AND MIRRORS MAKE THE MOST OF NATURAL LIGHT.

AFFIXING THE NICKEL SCONCE DIRECTLY TO THE MIRROR PROVIDES PRACTICAL TASK LIGHTING AND DOUBLES THE DECORATIVE EFFECT OF THE SHAPE.

"The most important thing for me was to take advantage of light coming in," Dahlman says. "That was crucial—capturing the light."

Contrasting textures add interest to a neutral color scheme. Gleaming ceramic tile frames the tub and mirrors, including a 10-foot-high vanity mirror bordered by elegant cornice tile molding. The floor's Botticino Fiorito marble tiles, stripped of their sheen, effect a stone texture to counterbalance the polish of the high-gloss decor.

The tub and shower work in concert to make a bathing space that befits the rest of the room. A deck of Italian

ITALIAN MARBLE SURROUNDS THE WHIRLPOOL TUB, CREATING A SUBSTANTIAL DECK THAT EXTENDS INTO THE SHOWER. THE BATH SURROUND SHOWCASES INTRICATE TILES THAT APPEAR HAND-CARVED.

ADORNED BY ELEGANT CERAMIC TILE, A HALF-WALL AND AN ARCH MAINTAIN AN UNHINDERED VIEW WHILE SUBTLY SEPARATING THE TOILET AREA FROM THE TUB.

marble surrounds the whirlpool tub and extends into the shower to create a bench. The recessed arched mirror that crowns the tub echoes the shape of the blue mosaic in the shower.

Continuing the continental flair, the spacious 10-foot-long vanity features two porcelain basins with European-style faucets. Cream-color paint blended with umber glaze gives the custom cabinet an antique appearance. A slab of marble tops the vanity.

An elegant sitting area near the window offers a cushioned bench for soaking in ample sunlight and viewing the countryside's green hills. The woven bamboo shades can be lowered to allow privacy when dressing.

With picturesque surroundings visible from almost anywhere in the room, it's no wonder the view inspired Dahlman's choices for the color palette. "I chose the colors to be very soothing and classic," Dahlman says of the natural tones and ivory that soften the room's structural grandeur.

Satin-nickel faucets with crystal handles suggest a vintage European style.

Crystal pulls on the vanity drawers maintain a sense of antique elegance while echoing the basins' crystal-handle faucets.

Aged with an umber glaze, the new vanity pairs contemporary functionality with antique details. Its front line curves to accentuate the two sink areas.

Bath and Breakfast

While Cyd and Steve Swerdlow were eager to create a spacious new master bath, they were stopped short by their home's layout. The 1941 center-hall colonial home's architecture offered plenty of charming style, but little room on the upper level to stretch.

After examining the sunroom off the main level, the Swerdlows' architect and designer had an expansive, sunny idea. "We could not figure out how to add on a nice, sizeable master bath," Cyd says. "They had the terrific idea to go out over the sunroom." With a sunny breakfast nook added to a newly elongated bath, the resulting room is a splendid domestic fusion of luxurious bathing and tableside relaxation.

Evoking the warm, aged tone of Tuscany, dark, stately marble graces the tub enclosure and vanity counter. Golden, dusty-color paint and tile create an antique sensibility on the walls, floor, and wainscoting. Distressed, cream-toned cabinetry suggests the comfortable cordiality of an aged villa. Reinforcing the classical references, marble columns frame the tub enclosure and repeat in the medicine cabinet. "I love to pamper myself," Cyd admits when talking about the Italian style. "We wanted a romantic place where we could luxuriate."

Small details provide convenience, comfort, and help establish the room's style. A tile-lined niche in the wall provides easy storage and builds the Old World feeling. Cross-handle nickel faucets provide an elegant, vintage touch, while a handmade area rug serves as a soothing, textured foundation. Radiant heat flooring and built-in stereo speakers deliver final elements of modern luxury. "Everything is about the mood," Cyd notes.

Adding an extra level of domestic convenience, the bath connects to a new small sunroom directly above the sunroom on the main floor. Featuring cabinets, counters, and appliances, the space functions as a small, bright breakfast nook or a relaxing point for evening contemplation. The combination of bath and sunroom suits the

INSPIRED BY CLASSICAL TUSCAN STYLE, THE ROOM'S DESIGN FEATURES EARTHY COLORS, MARBLE, CERAMIC TILE, AND COLUMNLIKE DETAILS. FRENCH DOORS LEAD TO A SUNROOM WHERE THE HOMEOWNERS CAN ENJOY A SUNLIT BREAKFAST.

couple's busy lives since Steve may rise early, shower, dress, and eat breakfast without leaving the master bath area or disturbing the rest of the household.

With three walls of windows, natural light floods the nook and continues through two French doors to illuminate the bath area. Convenient and elegant, the new space evokes the charm of Tuscany and provides all the comforts of home. "We can pamper ourselves in a sumptuous, soothing space," Cyd observes. "That's something we all deserve to do."

It might be minimal, but David O'Neil's master bath suite is far from boring. The bath, leisurely splashed across two upstairs rooms in David's historic Atlanta home, eschews ornamentation for clean, cool finishes that envelop bathers in elegance and luxury. "I wanted to use simple elements rather than flood your eyes," David says.

David gets his fill of color and pattern during the day as president of Renaissance Tile & Bath, so he wanted his bath to be a sleek, simple space that maximized light. To that end, he transformed a bedroom and sleeping porch into a two-room bathroom suite. One room serves as home to sinks, a shower, toilet, and bidet; the former sleeping porch houses the bathtub.

In the middle of one room the graceful, flattened-out bowls of dual Philippe Starck sinks hover on top of an antique Indonesian table. David had to assure the contractors that he really did want holes cut into the lovely old table. It's an unusual placement for a typical bath-room feature: David can walk around the vanity, stopping for a rest in a cocoa-brown chair nestled against a tall wooden dresser. No mirrors hang over the sinks; instead, a full-length, silver-framed mirror nestles against a wall, reflecting the shape of the window.

Behind the sinks, glass frames the front of a generous shower. In between shower and sleek bidet and toilet (also designed by Starck), a niche cleverly hides a tall wooden storage dresser. Subway-patterned tile continues

TWO ROOMS IN DAVID'S HISTORIC HOME WERE RECON-FIGURED INTO A SPACIOUS MASTER BATH SUITE.

SURROUNDED BY WINDOWS, BATHING IS NEARLY AN OUTSIDE EXPERIENCE.

higher than traditional wainscot height, covering two-thirds of the walls and topped by smaller tile squares and tile molding. Large limestone tiles serve as flooring in the vanity room.

A pair of doors, topped by a transom window, lead to the window-wrapped bathing space; the floor in that room transitions to a herringbone-patterned tile. The massive soaking tub, a custom-made reproduction of one from Paris, suspended on slightly curving feet, fills the room. A rolling bath cart and open shelves maintain the tub's unobstructed view. The gracefully arced faucet, a shape also found in the sink fixtures, provides the room's only decoration. Bathing on the former porch is "almost like being outside," David says.

Pared down to its essence, the room has the look of an expensive European hotel. "The way it is now is good," David says, "because there's not a lot of stuff around you to confuse your eye."

IN BETWEEN SHOWER, TOILET, AND BIDET, A NICHE HOLDS A TALL DRESSER FOR STORAGE. SLEEK FAUCETS CURVE ELEGANTLY ABOVE FLATTENED-OUT SINK BOWLS.

SIMPLE OPEN SHELVES LEAN AGAINST THE WALL IN THE SLEEPING PORCH. EXCEPT FOR A SMALL CART, THE ROOM IS UNENCUMBERED BY CLUTTER.

SPARKLING FAUCETS PROVIDE THE BATH WITH ITS SOLE DECORATION.

GRACEFUL FEET SUSPEND THE TUB ABOVE HERRING-BONE-PATTERNED TILES.

3 ASIAN INFLUENCE

Instill a tranquil, meditative quality in your bath with an Asian-inspired design. Use natural materials such as slate, soapstone, and lime-stone. Introducing wood elements or sea-grass wall coverings creates a harmonious blend of textures and materials. To counterpoint rougher textures add smooth glass and water-inspired, soothing colors such as aqua blue or sage green. Japanese soaking tubs enhance the spalike experience; many can be customized to accom-modate individual bathing preferences such as reclining or sitting while bathing. Place a teak bench in the shower area to enhance your enjoy-ment of a refreshing shower.

A Touch of Japan

It isn't often that a guest bathroom seduces homeowners to leave the comforts of their own retreat. But the Japanese influences in Rick Koffey and Barbara Thrasher's getaway suite may have done just that.

Architect Jeffrey Luth and interior designer Judy Davison created an understated, disciplined room that incorporates Japanese serenity and simplicity. Living and bathing areas flow into each other in the space, designed for hospitality and located atop the couple's Mercer Island, Washington, backyard garage.

The room's focal point is the deep, expansive Japanese soaking tub. Custom made of travertine slabs, the tub enjoys views of both Mount Rainier and the living room fireplace. A sliding shoji screen of imported Japanese sen wood separates it from the rest of the room.

Travertine appears again on the vanity countertop; its warm, organic colors perfectly complement the bluestone floor. The deep hue of the sculpturelike custom-cast bronze sink accents the horizontal lines and muted warmth of the woven raffia wall covering. A solid wall hides a private bathroom shower and toilet.

With its majestic views and tranquil design, the suite attracts its share of visitors—particularly the couple, who steal away for a soak when the room is empty. "Our guests are overwhelmed with the details here," Barbara says. "The surprises just unfold the longer they stay."

NATURAL MATERIALS—THE WOVEN RAFFIA WALL COVERING, THE TRAVERTINE COUNTERTOP, AND THE SEN WOOD SHOJI SCREEN AND VANITY BASE—CONSTITUTE IMPORTANT JAPANESE DESIGN ELEMENTS.

WHEN THE SHOJI SCREEN IS OPEN, UNOBSTRUCTED VIEWS FROM THE SOAKING TUB LOOK OUTWARD TO MOUNT RAINIER OR INWARD TO THE LIVING ROOM FIREPLACE.

STYLIZED BUILDER'S-GRADE VANITY MIRROR
FRAMED PRINTS PUNCH UP TUB SURROUND
CORDING DEFINES EDGES ON WALLS AND CEILINGS
SIXTEENTH-CENTURY CHEST FOR STORAGE

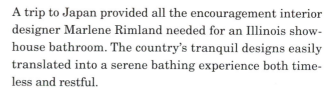

A trip to Japan provided all the encouragement interior designer Marlene Rimland needed for an Illinois show-house bathroom. The country's tranquil designs easily translated into a serene bathing experience both time-less and restful.

The room groups a tub and toilet in one space; a sepa-rate alcove contains a sink and vanity. Rimland replaced the all-white space with a textural paint treatment, pro-viding a background for fixtures and fabrics. A shade of warm red fills the alcove; the room's remaining white walls are covered in a dark tan. The cool combination has just enough punch, and combed glazes add an exotic sur-face finish.

In the tub room, matchstick blinds shield the window from view, while hand-painted silk panels mimic ancient scrolls. An elegantly framed surround dresses up the plain-white tub. Its front panels became focal points with the addition of Japanese-inspired prints.

Rimland took advantage of easy, affordable bathroom pieces, dressing them up for style. A framed mirror hangs directly over a standard builder-grade vanity mirror for a unique touch. "The second mirror makes it more elegant, and the cording and rosette [from which the mirror hangs] add another decorative element," Rimland says.

The perfect finishing touch to the restful, Far East style came with a 16th-century chest that sits in the alcove. "Everyone just loved the look and feel of this bathroom," Rimland says.

THE BAMBOOLIKE FRAME ON A SECOND, SMALLER MIRROR PLACED ATOP THE VANITY MIRROR CONTIN-UES THE RESTFUL ASIAN DESIGN THEME. CORDING IN THE CORNERS OF THE ALCOVE DEFINES THE EDGES AND ADDS JUST A HINT OF DRAMA.

A METAL STAND BETWEEN TUB AND TOILET HOLDS TOWELS AND CANDLES. HEAVY-DUTY HOOK-AND-LOOP FASTENING TAPE SECURES THE PRINTS TO THE TUB SURROUND. A TATAMI-STYLE BATH MAT WARMS THE WHITE TILE FLOOR.

FINDING ZEN

The colors, lines, and textures of nature and modern design find balance and Zenlike calm in the master bath for a California showhouse.

The room's Asian references come from a streamlined bed in the adjoining bedroom. Interior designer Gene Zettle left behind his original inspiration to layer the bathroom walls completely in stone. Instead limestone tiles come to wainscot level; above that handmade rice paper textured with real bamboo leaves covers the upper portion. The smooth texture of the lower half juxtaposes nicely against the rippled layers of the paper.

Horizontal bands of green kirkstone—a volcanic rock—mark the breaks between paper, limestone, and baseboards. Dark accents, echoing the color of the bamboo leaves, run across the floor and around the shower's door frame, balancing the large swaths of the room's cool creamy tones.

A 19th-century Chinese chest turned vanity allows ample room for bathroom functions and enlivens the space without overpowering it. Topped with a limestone slab, marble above-counter bowl-style sink, and sleek contemporary faucet, the composition perfectly offsets the bathroom's aesthetic atmosphere. Wall sconces above the wide mirror cast soft light on the surface below. The design comes full circle with two rows of simply framed, simply rendered vintage botanical prints.

"The bathroom turned out very inviting," Zettle says. "The materials blended nicely, and everything felt right."

VINTAGE BOTANICAL PRINTS ECHO THE REAL BAMBOO LEAVES EMBEDDED IN THE WALL'S RICE PAPER. THE FLOOR'S LIMESTONE GRID IS CRISSCROSSED BY THE SAME COLOR THAT FRAMES THE BASEBOARDS.

TOPPED WITH A MARBLE SINK AND SLEEK FAUCET, THE VANITY IS THE ROOM'S CENTERPIECE, CUEING THE DARK ACCENTS IN FLOORS AND WALLS.

SERENE SOAK

She savors a soothing bath. He enjoys the steam of a shower. Ensconced in soapy suds, she desires nothing more than a glass of wine, candles, and a book to enjoy in a good, long soak. He favors a pelting rain of water to ease bicycling aches. Both disparate bathing styles unite equally in Susan and Richard Newhauser's stylishly outfitted master bath.

It was a remodeling project that began with good bones: The couple's home was designed and originally owned by Florence Knoll of Knoll furniture fame. During a whole-house remodel the Newhausers turned to interior designer Michael Wolk, with the caveat to retain the home's contemporary 1970s look. "We basically gutted the house, but came up with a design that respected the home's architecture," says Wolk, who collaborated with project designer Roxana Matticoli on the bath's design.

At some point in the house's history that room had been divided into two smaller baths. The Newhausers recombined the space in a clever plan that incorporates geometric forms with elegantly simple materials and gives them views of a lush garden, billowing palm trees, and Biscayne Bay.

The room's design is simple, accented with equally tasteful finishes. Fixtures in the 17×14-rectangle orient around a half-wall that divides the soaking tub from the rest of the space. The tub faces large windows looking onto the bay, but the limestone-fronted wall is a privacy partition that doesn't block the light or the views for the rest of the room. On the other side of the wall sits a toilet compartment, shower, and shared double sink.

Limestone clads most of the room and forms the basis of many fixtures; a bit of glass, a few mirrors, a little stainless steel, and sleek faucets supply just enough contrast. "The walls, floors, sink, and tub are all created from slabs of limestone," Wolk says. "We chose limestone because of how it felt to the touch, its beautiful warmth, and its subtle graining pattern that works well with more modern designs."

The custom limestone trough sink faces the shower and toilet compartment. While the sink is communal in character, double faucets and individual prep stations carved out of the divider wall allow separate grooming

THE CONSISTENT COLOR OF THE LIMESTONE, WHICH TRANSITIONS SEAMLESSLY FROM FLOOR TO DIVIDER WALL TO SINK, IS A SERENE BACKDROP TO THE BATHING HAVEN.

space. Each has a mirror set into a notch in the wall and a deep ledge for toiletries.

In an unusual twist, a trio of stainless-steel cabinets perpendicular to the divider accommodate storage for bathing necessities. Inset into the thick exterior wall, their frames and adjustable glass shelves don't detract from the room's simple, stylish elegance. "We wanted the sink and mirrors to stand alone, so the built-in cabinets were a nice way to keep daily necessities within reach, but behind enclosures that are more interesting when they're lit from within," Susan says.

Inside the enclosed shower, a long vertical window opens onto the private front courtyard. Glass shower doors allow in light and views, and counterbalance a similar toilet compartment across the room. The sweep of stone makes a seamless transition to the soaking tub, which not only was contoured to the couple's reclining bodies but also adjusted for their heights and individual

SET INTO AN EXTERIOR WALL, STAINLESS-STEEL STORAGE CABINETS ARE SLEEK AND PRACTICAL.

WITH STEPS DOWN INTO ITS CUSTOM-CONTOURED SPACE, THE LIMESTONE SOAKING TUB STAYS PRIVATE BEHIND THE HALF-WALL. DAY OR NIGHT, VIEWS INTO THE BAY BEYOND FURNISH A PEACEFUL CANVAS.

views of the backyard lap pool and waves in the bay.

With its earthen texture and subtle color variations, limestone is the perfect refined backdrop for the room's organic sophistication. "I love bathing in a Japanese way: in a steaming, soaking bath without the noise of whirlpool jets," Susan says. "When I get the candles going, I feel like I'm in my own little retreat. The bath has a beautiful inside-out feeling, which we both love."

GLASS ENCLOSES THE SHOWER AND TOILET COMPARTMENT; A LONG, TALL WINDOW LOOKS OUT ONTO TROPICAL VIEWS.

SEPARATE GROOMING STATIONS WITH DEEP LEDGES ALLOW A MODICUM OF PRIVACY. THE TROUGH SINK IS THE PERFECT COMPANION FOR A SHARED BATH.

INSIDE THE SHOWER A NICHE AND MIRROR ALLOW RICHARD SHAVING SPACE.

Purifying Waters

Seeking a serene, flowing balance, this small bath finds harmony in the organic partnership of earth and water. Simple, nature-inspired choices give these homeowners a soothing, uncluttered space in a limited area.

The room's elemental fusion is dominated by a wall covered entirely with blue-tinted glass tiles. This subdued, enchanting feature disperses light throughout the room and produces the sense of a cascading waterfall. On the opposing wall, muted green paint counters the blue glass and its shimmering effect. With delicate, sand-hued limestone on the floor, the combination of elements creates a sealike convergence of colors.

River pebbles set in mortar form the shower floor. The shower enclosure uses one open side and one clear glass wall to maintain a fluid sense of openness. Influenced by Asian designs, the tub and sink are supported by dark Java wood frames, providing visually heavy, yet elegant, features.

A broad window provides natural illumination and creates an invigorating, kinetic atmosphere. Along with the cascading wall of glass, reflective elements such as mirrors and chrome faucets disperse light throughout the room. With this interplay of light and color, the room produces a glimmering sense of water as it flows through a clear, serene landscape.

Natural light streaming in from the window creates a bright, invigorating effect with the color scheme, while the Asian-inspired sink frame provides a heavy visual anchor.

Resembling a streambed or tidal pool, the shower floor is composed of river pebbles set in mortar.

Blue-tinted glass tile creates a cascading combination of light and color, while the shower's glass wall allows the effect to flow unhindered throughout the room.

Meditative Moments

Judy and Frank Coyle looked to an ancient culture to create a tranquil escape that conveys their passion for Japanese design. "The whole point of the bath design was to create a peaceful retreat and respite from a busy world," Judy says.

For their master bath the couple already had a collection of Japanese objects, which are now displayed on shelves above the tub. For further inspiration the couple visited Japan, searching out ideas, taking notes, and deciding on surface and lighting design.

Frank wanted a Japanese soaking tub in the 600-square-foot room. "I thought that sounded like a maintenance nightmare," Judy says. "We couldn't have that and a regular tub, so we found a stainless-steel soaking tub that we could have customized to fit both of us." The tub is contoured to allow Frank to sit on his side, and Judy's side slopes so she can recline.

Customizing other features in the bath helped create a personalized spalike retreat. Two showerheads are installed at different heights in the tiled walk-in shower, and a pair of commode closets and separate vanities allow the room to function for both simultaneously.

The blend of textures and natural materials further enhances the meditative Japanese atmosphere. Flat-back river rocks adhered to a mesh backing adorn the shower floor; slate tiles line the shower walls and the floor throughout. The counter and tub surround are soapstone. To further the meditative, earthy feel, the walls are painted sage green. "It's the blending of textures that gives the room an earthiness that has a calming energy," says interior designer Terry Terry, who worked with a feng shui consultant on design details.

A happy coincidence provided the final Japanese detail in the room: "The light hits in such a way that it creates a shadow kimono above the tub," Terry says. "It was the perfect finishing touch, and we couldn't have planned it if we tried."

Slate tiles, a soapstone counter, and sage green walls create a relaxing, Zenlike space.

Tucked behind the wall housing the vanity, the slate-tile shower functions without a door.

Slate tiles surround a mosaic of river rock with a natural, nonslip texture. A teak bench offers another earthy element.

Towels perch on stainless-steel hooks just inside the glass-panel entry of the slate-tiled shower.

Dark soapstone countertops create striking visual contrast with sage green walls and collectibles.

Japanese objects rest on shelves above the stainless-steel tub, which was customized to fit the couple's differing tastes.

4 TRADITIONAL STYLE

Combine the warmth and luxury of traditional features, such as furniture-style cabinets, crown moldings, and architectural details with pampering amenities such as whirlpool tubs, heated towel bars, and radiant heat floors, and it's easy to understand why traditional decor is never out of style. These baths are far from stuffy; they're indulgently comfortable and accommodating. Honed marble, glazed paint finishes, and glass-paneled cabinet doors contribute to the theme. Look to a bump-out bay window to provide space for a soaking tub or whirlpool bath. Incorporate separate compartments for toilet and bidet, shower, and grooming areas for the privacy of two bathers.

Vanity Flair

Lack of storage space may reduce even the most elegant bath to an impractical morass of clutter. Maggie and Lew Bellville feared that limited storage would mean a complete remodeling of their Atlanta home's master bath.

Happily for the couple, interior designer Teri Duffy's approach allowed the room to keep most of its original structure and dramatically enhance its stately beauty. She intended to find a substantial amount of storage and still, as she notes, "create something that was much prettier than a utilitarian closet."

Duffy's plan is a grand floor-to-ceiling, wall-length vanity that redefines the room's ornate sensibility. "Because it would be seen from the bedroom, I knew I wanted it to look like furniture," Duffy says.

Along with a broad swath of drawers, the vanity features cabinets with glass doors reaching to the ceiling. The array of shelving ensures vast amounts of organized storage without sacrificing style. Fluted details on columnlike dividers introduce a grand elegance for the cabinets. Capped by deep crown molding, the glass cabinets frame a large three-piece mirror. The mirror is bridged by a subtly arched facade that hides task lighting and softens the cabinets' towering influence.

A HAMMERED-METAL SINK CREATES HANDCRAFTED BEAUTY AND PROVIDES A REFLECTIVE ELEMENT TO THE ONYX COUNTERTOP.

CUSTOM-MADE CABINETS OFFER MORE THAN AMPLE STORAGE WHILE FABRIC LININGS ELIMINATE EXPOSING A CLUTTERED SHELF.

BESIDES PROVIDING A BROAD SPACE FOR STORAGE, THE CABINETRY REINFORCES A SENSE OF AGED ELEGANCE WITH ANTIQUED GLAZE AND FURNITURE-LIKE DETAILING.

FURNITURELIKE CABINETRY
FABRIC-LINED GLASS DOORS
LEADED-GLASS WINDOWS

While the need for storage inspired the cabinetry, the vanity endows the room with an Old World ambience. On the cabinets, a brown glaze tops a languid, buttery gold paint, creating a hint of age. Honey-tone onyx forms the countertop, and a striking, hammered-metal bowl creates a handcrafted feel to the sink. "We didn't want the bathroom to look too new, too crisp," Duffy notes.

Restraining the vanity's dominance, limestone flooring instills an earthy, muted foundation. Soft curtains of green fabric line the glass cabinet doors and add a counterpoint of color. "The fabric helps break up all the wood," Duffy says, "making it lighter-feeling and adding color."

Balancing the wall-length vanity is the whirlpool tub, graced by an ornate, leaded-glass window. The elegant glass feature is opaque at the bottom for privacy. Eventually it becomes clearer at the top, allowing a bather to luxuriate in natural light.

For these homeowners a need for more storage led to an elegant revelation with minimal remodeling. Function and refinement coalesce in grandly constructed cabinetry that redefines the entire bath. As Duffy contends, "This design makes it so much warmer and approachable than a plain old vanity."

AN ARCHED FASCIA HIDES LIGHTING, FRAMES THE MIRRORS, AND MUTES TOWERING CABINETS.

A TALL, ORNATE, LEADED-GLASS WINDOW SERVES AS A DECORATIVE BACKDROP, ALLOWING PRIVACY AND NATURAL ILLUMINATION.

HIGH ABOVE THE COUNTERTOP SELDOM-USED ITEMS FIND A PLACE IN THE UPPERMOST CABINET SHELVES.

BLANK CANVAS

Bob and Karen Hoehn avoided the impulse to fill their master bath with unnecessary decoration and frivolous color. Instead the room's neutral palette combined with an ingenious use of architectural details forms a spacious, stylish retreat.

A creamy color scheme sets the backdrop for the L-shape room, broken into a 7×9-foot dressing area, a 12×7-foot bathing area, and a commode room. The palette gave Karen exactly the scheme she wanted. "Monochromatic and light colors make it appear a lot larger than it is," she says.

In the bathing area the couple and architect Richard Bokal chose slabs of honed travertine for every surface, from ceiling to walls, custom-made tub, and floor. Clear sealant waterproofed the porous material but maintained its natural appeal; the tub in particular looks almost sculptural. Light bounces through the tub's window, sandblasted at the bottom, and past a frameless glass wall that encloses the combination bathtub and shower. The treatment avoids the fussiness of a traditional shower curtain or mottled door.

A wide archway between bathing and dressing areas defines the two spaces, but eliminates the need for a door. Its ledge, also topped with travertine, is both a divider and visual treat. It has just enough space for Karen to exercise some of her decorating style, with a burst of color, a vase, or well-chosen seashell. "There's always something flowering on the ledge," she says. "I usually have a bright-color orchid sitting there, or tulips."

Mirrors and mirrored medicine cabinets fill the wall above the dual vanity sinks, bouncing light further into the space and doubling its visual size. Travertine forms a backsplash and tops the neutral white cabinets. Covered by a simple roller shade, a center window looks into the adjacent interior atrium. The dark wood floor, continued

BETWEEN THE DUAL SINKS, A ROLLER SHADE SHIELDS AN INTERIOR ATRIUM, ALLOWING IN EVEN MORE LIGHT.

TRAVERTINE FOR WALLS, FLOORS, AND TUB
ARCHWAY LEDGE INSTEAD OF A DOOR
FRAMELESS GLASS WALL ENCLOSES SHOWER
MIRRORS TO DOUBLE VISUAL SPACE

from the master bedroom, balances the bursts of sunlight and creamy colors.

The clean lines allow Karen and Bob endless decorating possibilities, particularly with accents. Favored prints from their art collection hang at opposite ends of the space, one in the commode room and the other at the dressing area entrance. Metal-and-crackle-glass sconces, made by a local artist, hang above the dual sinks and act as visual sculpture. "The interest comes in the accessories," Karen says.

The finished master bath is no exception to the rest of the couple's minimal, classic style. "There's nothing ornate in our house," Karen says.

An archway serves as an architectural element, defining the break between the couple's bathing and dressing areas.

Simple silver pulls on cabinet doors and drawers are part of the neutral palette. An Asian-style vase and framed print add a dash of color.

A clear sealant protects the travertine's pitted, beige surface. A window, sandblasted at the bottom, hides the view from outside.

For Theresa and Richard Davis necessity proved to be the mother of remodeling invention. Attempting to update their 1910 home, they discovered a load-bearing wall precisely where they were about to expand the master bath. Rather than abandon their plans, the couple became creative. "At 11 o' clock at night," Theresa recalls, "we took black markers and drew a new design plan out on the floor."

Instead of being an obstacle, the inconvenient wall served as a prime source of inspiration, becoming the divider in a two-part bath. The wall remained, and the adjacent room—a previously unused guest bedroom—

was divided into the new bath extension and a spacious walk-in closet.

The transformation proved a simple and elegant solution to the couple's constricted space. The old bathroom now contains the toilet area and a gracious vanity with stately cherry cabinetry. Designer Karen Bieszerzak selected the cherry to coordinate with the old home. "The cherry adds richness to the bath," Bieszerzak says. "There is enough natural and artificial light in the space that it doesn't feel heavy at all."

Through a new doorway and on the other side of the barrier wall, a new room contains the tub and walk-in shower. The new shower space offers a luxurious water massage, with several showerheads mounted on the sidewalls. On the opposite wall and tucked beneath a window, the tub delivers more traditional, serene amenities such as a restful view of the wooded surroundings.

The redefined spaces share sand-colored tiles on the tub and shower surrounds as well as on the heated floor. The soothing earth tones repeat in a striated finish on the walls. To further lighten the ambience, ivory highlights the woodwork, vanity countertop, and tub.

The balance found in design also finds its way into the couple's lives. With a new wall and doorway from the bathing area, the remains of the former bedroom serve as a spacious walk-in closet for Richard. Here he prepares for his day, which begins much earlier than Theresa's. "We didn't want to have Richard's closet in the master bedroom itself," Theresa admits. "This way all his things are in the bathroom area, and he doesn't disturb me while I'm sleeping."

For the Davis household, a happy accident of architecture and a little creativity led to a perfect balance. "This project started off badly," Theresa reflects. "Now it is just total relaxation."

CONNECTED BY A NEW PASSAGEWAY FROM THE VANITY ROOM, A PREVIOUSLY UNUSED BEDROOM IS DIVIDED TO CREATE A BATHING AREA AND AN EXPANSIVE WALK-IN CLOSET.

THE BATHTUB AFFORDS A PEACEFUL VIEW OF THE SURROUNDING WOODS.

Countering the predominantly light color scheme, a dark cherry vanity gives rich warmth to a newly redefined space.

The new walk-in shower features side-mounted showerheads for steam and pulsing massage.

Bathing Bay

No windows and poor ventilation yield ugly and uncomfortable consequences in the humid environment of a master bath, a problem Peggy and Joe Jester faced in their home. "Our old bathroom was moldy and mildewed," Peggy recalls. The space was not only dark, but also small and short on storage. Plus, the old tub-shower combination lacked the efficiency, spaciousness, and good looks that a separate bathtub and shower could provide.

Situated on a large wooded lot, the Jester's home features a rear facade that faces south. The couple concluded that the room's location at the back of the house made it an ideal candidate for expansion. "We knew the southern exposure would give us a lot of light," Peggy says, "and that putting windows all around the addition would also provide good ventilation."

Opening up the back wall of the bathroom made way

SQUARE TRANSOMS ABOVE CASEMENTS EMPHASIZE THE DRAMATIC CEILING HEIGHT OF THE MASTER BATH. OPERATED BY REMOTE CONTROL, CELLULAR WINDOW SHADES CAN BE LOWERED FOR PRIVACY.

A 6-FOOT-LONG COPPER PLANTER INSET INTO THE TUB SURROUND INTRODUCES A TOUCH OF GREEN TO THE BATHROOM. THE PLANTS SOAK UP PLENTY OF NATURAL LIGHT THROUGH THE WINDOWS.

WHITE 4×4-INCH TILES LINE THE WALK-IN SHOWER, AUGMENTING THE ROOM'S SUNNY DISPOSITION.

THE COLOR OF THE WARM YELLOW WALLS WAS CUSTOM-MADE BY ADDING UMBER COLOR TO PURCHASED WALL PAINT. A WHITEWASHED CHAIR PAIRED WITH WHITE TOWELS, WOODWORK, AND TILES PLAYS OFF THE WALLS.

THE TWO VANITIES ARE TOPPED WITH WHITE SOLID SURFACING THE SAME COLOR AS THE MIRROR FRAME AND WAINSCOTING AROUND THE WINDOWS. A FREE-STANDING STORAGE CUPBOARD IN THE TOILET COMPARTMENT MIMICS THE VANITIES' STYLE.

for a 19-foot-wide addition that intersects the old space like the top of a T. Breaking through the standard-height ceiling allowed both the old and new spaces to soar to 10½ feet.

Highlighting the addition is the window-wrapped bay that reaches out toward the woods. Five tall windows above the tub flood the room with light and showcase a scenic wooded setting. A large whirlpool tub nestles into the bay, creating the ultimate spot to unwind and rest weary muscles.

Two compartments flank the bay window—one for a walk-in shower and the other for the toilet. Partial walls lend privacy to both areas. "Leaving off the doors makes the shower and toilet more accessible," Peggy says. "Plus,

the shower is large enough that water doesn't splash out of the entry, and there's no shower door to clean."

The original bath forms the stem of the new T-shape room. In this area a roomy walk-in closet replaced the space once occupied by the tub-shower unit, a small vanity, and the toilet. By annexing two small closets, the Jesters also created a space for a pair of long white

vanities on opposite walls.

To finish the room, Peggy chose textured, buttery-tan 12×12-inch tiles and a radiant heating system for the floor. A timer turns the heating system on in the morning. The soft yellow paint on the walls adds to the warmth of the floor, creating a glow that makes the room cheerful even on gloomy days.

Delft Delight

For master ceramist, painter, and sculptor Anne Coke, making a new master bath meant creating both a practical, usable space and a work of artistic expression.

After sharing a bath "the size of a closet" for 44 years with her husband, Henry, Anne produced a bath that's all her own. A new addition includes a walk-in shower, single-sink vanity, enclosed toilet compartment, and a dressing area with custom-made cabinets. While these elements are not unusual for a new bathroom, the decor is unique to the homeowner.

Embracing her love of blue-and-white delft porcelain, Anne produced two elaborate murals in the shower, painting, glazing, and firing all of the tiles herself. Extending the charming theme throughout the room, painted butterflies adorn the sink, flowerpots, and even a ceramic tissue holder.

Thanks to a sandblasted, leaded-glass window and French doors that open to a private courtyard, natural light illuminates the charming decor.

In its final form the bath is a fully realized presentation of Anne's artistic vision within a physical space. In fact a Latin phrase painted on the medicine cabinet reminds her of this harmony every day: *Mens sana corpore sano*. "A sound mind in a sound body."

HAND-PAINTED BUTTERFLIES IN A SINK GLAZED AND FIRED BY THE HOMEOWNER EXTEND THE DELFT BLUE THEME TO THE VANITY.

FEATURING PICKLED OAK WOOD AND A PEWTER-FINISHED FAUCET, THE VANITY ESTABLISHES A COMFORTABLE CHARM. THE FRENCH DOORS OPEN ONTO A PRIVATE COURTYARD.

SERVING AS THE CENTRAL FEATURE OF THE ROOM AND INSPIRED BY DELFT BLUE ENGLISH PORCELAIN, HOMEOWNER ANNE COKE DESIGNED, PAINTED, GLAZED, AND FIRED ALL OF THE TILES.

Hand-painted tile and sink
Leaded-glass windows with blue border
Tile murals for the shower enclosure

LIFETIME LUXURY

When Karen and Jay Flynn first bought their starter home in a peaceful, wooded Pittsburgh neighborhood, they embraced its coziness and the charm of the area. Twenty years and one son later, the space is no longer cozy, but constricting. In the past each time the couple considered moving, they remained loyal to their little home, once expanding the kitchen. This time they decided to remain for the long haul and remodeled the home to encompass both their new tastes and their future needs. As Karen says, the new work would let the couple remain "for as long as we can possibly foresee."

Architect Susan Tusick knew the remodeling job would alter almost every area of the home and represent a dramatic reinterpretation of the space. With the future in mind, the homeowners wanted a luxurious master bath for themselves and a design that considered accessibility for those with impaired mobility. Before their remodeling project had begun, Karen's father had become wheelchair-bound, and the couple realized that accessibility was an immediate priority for her parents and a possible

Natural light soothingly illuminates the room through a grand, arch-topped window.

After 20 years of constricted, shared space, this new master bath offers soothing luxuries, including a generous, inviting tub.

The substantial tub enclosure is wide enough to hold a book or a cup of morning coffee.

future issue for themselves.

Confronting the issue of space, the new master bath is part of a new addition that extends from the upper level and is cantilevelered over the hillside lot. A peaked ceiling creates a graceful, centralized space for a broad installation of windows. Dominated by a grand, Palladian-style window with its pleasing arch, the windows create an entrance for soothing natural light and a view of the surrounding magnolia trees. "It's like a treehouse," Karen says.

Replicating the spalike styles they had seen on a trip to Europe, marblelike ceramic tile laid diagonally across the floor extends up the wall. An ornate frieze design across the top highlights the Old World elegance.

Utilizing the extra space, a luxurious tub anchors the room. Ceramic tile that surrounds the tub enclosure is wide enough to serve as a convenient book rest, place for coffee, or a bench when entering or exiting the bath. Importantly for the couple, the tub's relaxing occupant may recline and look directly out the new windows.

Simple details help complete the couple's dream bath. Featuring muted, soothing green tones, the two clean-lined vanities and a narrow closet provide substantial and elegantly unobtrusive storage. An enclosure hides both a toilet and bidet; the new shower is broad and spacious. Radiant floor heating warms the tiles, and a stereo system Jay installed provides added ambience.

"I love to come up here at night, close the door, and turn the music on," Jay says. "Stresses of the day just melt away."

Having amply supplied the luxury, Susan Tusick also created accessibility without compromising style. The doors are a wheelchair-suitable 3 feet wide, and the vanities feature removable doors for roll-up use. In the closet the shelves are broad and shallow, permitting easy access for a seated person. At 3 feet 6 inches, the lighting

A PEAKED ROOF, BROAD WINDOWS, CLEAN-LINED FIXTURES, AND MUTED GREEN COLORS SET A SERENE, LUXURIOUS TONE.

DESPITE THE PRACTICAL, ACCESSIBLE DESIGN, THE ROOM IS DEFINED BY A EUROPEAN AMBIENCE OF LUXURY AND ELEGANCE.

controls are installed at a low, convenient height. Although the shower offers luxurious individual space, it is also large enough to accommodate a second person for assistance, and it features a removable threshold for roll-in access.

Having remained loyal to their home, the Flynns have reconstructed a home that will remain loyal to them. Combining their desire for luxury and recognition for future practicality, this master bath will continue to grow with the couple far into the future.

"We dreamt of this place as a retreat that we'd enjoy every day," Karen says, "and when we close the doors, that's what it is."

THE TALL CLOSET PRESENTS A CLEAN, UNOBTRUSIVE APPEARANCE. SHELVES ARE SHALLOW AND ADJUSTABLE FOR EASY ACCESS.

WITH A WIDE DOOR, REMOVABLE THRESHOLD, AND A HANDHELD SPRAYER, THE AMPLE SHOWER ENCLOSURE OFFERS PERSONAL COMFORT AND EASY ACCESS.

MARBLELIKE CERAMIC TILE WITH AN ORNATE FRIEZE DESIGN EVOKES THE SOPHISTICATED FEEL OF AN ITALIAN SPA.

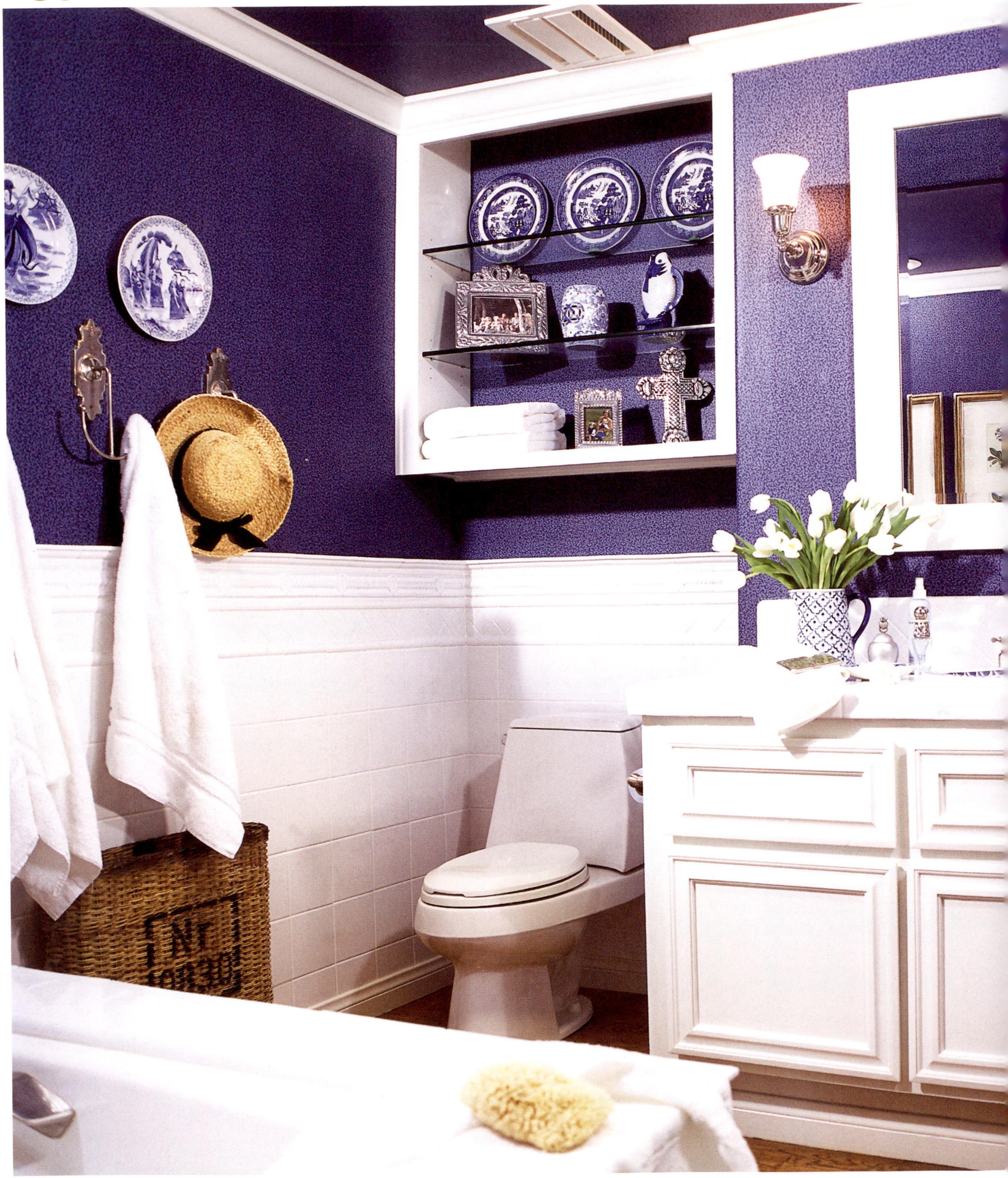

It isn't often that a collection forms the basis for a bathroom design. But in Sandy Dodge's home, her passions for French toile fabrics and English and Chinese porcelain were the perfect foundation for a revamped master bathroom. "Blue and white is just a color combination I've always loved," Sandy says. "It always seems to be fresh and crisp, and at the same time peaceful. Plus, it never seems to go out of style."

From delicately glazed plates to sturdy vases, framed botanical prints to silver crosses, Sandy's lovingly assembled menagerie was the perfect monogram for the small 15-year-old space, which measures just $8\frac{1}{2} \times 8$. A vanity and toilet sit directly across from the bathtub, and a door joins the bath with the master bedroom.

Interior designer Linda Kaufman used Sandy's collection and favorite colors as the basis for the design. In the nearly square space she added traditional wainscoting around most of the room; the crisp white ceramic tile and stacked ceramic moldings add architectural detail and texture. The small print in the deep blue curlicue-pattern wallpaper matches the hue in Sandy's collectible china. Crown molding in bright white marks the break between wall and true-blue ceiling.

Kaufman also took out an unnecessarily large shower stall, replacing it with a tub that looks and feels more spacious. A reproduction English-style faucet with a telephone-style handheld shower attachment completes the relaxing atmosphere.

To trim costs Kaufman recycled the original vanity cabinet, giving it new life with a coat of white paint, ceramic tile countertop, and new recessed-panel doors and drawers. A reproduction French-style faucet was installed directly into the countertop, while a French porcelain hand-painted sink adds another collectible element. Painted stock wood molding frames a large mirror, flanked by a pair of nickel-and-frosted-glass sconces.

With plenty of storage below the sink, a former linen cabinet was reincarnated as display space. With the

WITH STORAGE BELOW THE SINK, A FORMER LINEN CABINET BECAME DISPLAY SPACE; WOOD SHELVES WERE REPLACED WITH GLASS. WALLPAPER CONTINUES THE COLOR SCHEME.

doors removed and glass shelves replacing wood ones, the nook showcases select pieces from Sandy's collection, giving it special charm. Mounted above the tub, another small cupboard with a glass door—this one reminiscent of a medicine cabinet—holds several more items. "We had the luxury of using the cabinet as display space for more of Sandy's porcelain collection as well as some framed family photos," Kaufman says.

Behind both display cabinets the visible wallpaper continues the color scheme while emphasizing the collectibles. The decor meshes with the adjacent master bedroom, where toile patterns appear in fabrics and wall coverings. Gold leaf frames sparkle above the tub; space-smart pewter hooks replace towel bars. "With a hook, you don't have to fold the towels just-so to get them to look right, and I actually think they dry faster," Sandy says. "Besides, I think draped towels look more elegant and at the same time more relaxed. That was the kind of balance I was looking for in this bath."

An antique French porcelain sink is another piece in Sandy's collection. The nickel-plated faucet was set directly into the countertop.

A tub replaced a too-big shower. Added elegance comes from a nickel-plated, handheld shower attachment.

Sandy's revived bathroom was fashioned just like any other room—for utility and charm, function and character. Organized together, the collectibles, mementos, souvenirs, and artwork give the bath the individual stamp of its owner. "A bath isn't automatically off-limits to decorative objects that are personally appealing and meaningful," Kaufman says. "In fact those kinds of objects can help make a bath feel more gracious and less utilitarian."

Sandy's collection of pieces adds a touch of graciousness, and the things of beauty she loves gives this bathroom character and charm.

SPACE-SAVING PEWTER HOOKS TAKE UP LESS ROOM THAN TOWEL BARS. PIECES OF SANDY'S CHINA COLLECTION HANG ABOVE THE CRISP, WHITE TOWELS.

CERAMIC TILE WAINSCOTING AND MOLDING, AS WELL AS A WHITE CERAMIC TILE TUB SURROUND, ADD CLASSIC DETAILS. A GLASS-DOOR CABINET HOLDS EVEN MORE COLLECTIBLES.

Tranquil Tones

Although Pam Paniello embraces vibrant design in the rest of her house, soothing harmony was a necessity in her master bath. Rejecting excessive distractions, a neutral color palette of whites and yellows sets the tone for this restful space. A languid barrel-vaulted ceiling and a rounded vanity add soft architectural details to the harmonious tones. In a room that is intended to be an oasis of calm, Pam says, "It's important to have soft edges."

The ambience may be subdued, but it doesn't lack luxury. Richly veined marble graces the vanity countertop and the tub surround. The tub features a waterfall faucet, and the room offers two cedar closets.

Along with the serene colors and textures, a sense of openness contributes to the soothing effect. Preventing a boxed-in feel, the shower is open and, along with the toilet, defined only by low walls. Glass-paned French doors create an elegant entrance and allow a striking view of the graceful, arched window. The doors separate two van-

ities, which provide plenty of space for easy movement.

Fusing a calming palette and a breezy openness, this master bath creates a residential escape from the hectic world. "I feel it should be a tranquil retreat," Pam says. "It's one place you can go to rest and relax without a lot going on."

THE VANITY CABINET ECHOES THE SOFT, ROUNDED FEATURES FOUND ELSEWHERE IN THE ROOM. A LOW DIVIDER WALL MAINTAINS A SENSE OF OPENNESS IN THE SHOWER.

NESTLED BENEATH THE ARCHED WINDOW AND BARREL-VAULTED CEILING, THE TUB FEATURES A WATERFALL FAUCET AND DIVIDER WALLS WITH STORAGE NICHES.

VINTAGE VIEW

Valerie and Dave Lasker were in an enviable position. Their 1920s home possessed all the Edwardian charm and sophistication of San Francisco's Cow Hollow neighborhood. Furthermore, from a gracefully arched window they had a splendid view of panoramic San Francisco Bay. Unfortunately for the homeowners, this view was from their bedroom closet.

Frustratingly, the master bath adjacent to the closet possessed only a small window above the toilet that offered a slim view between neighboring buildings. The bath had other shortcomings, such as a constricted shower stall, a tub they seldom used, and most despairingly, the glossy remnants of a 1980s remodeling job. Eager to embrace the bay view and resurrect the room's

A FREESTANDING CABINET MAINTAINS A VINTAGE, FURNITURELIKE QUALITY, WITH ITS ROUNDED ELEMENTS AND QUEEN ANNE-STYLE FEET.

Vintage furniturelike vanity
Curved, clear shower enclosure
Tile wainscoting

heritage, Valerie, an interior designer, knew something had to change.

With the assistance of architect Thomas Knott, the couple formulated a plan for the bath and closet to swap spaces. Further, they planned to expand the new bathroom by annexing space from a dressing area and the master bedroom. To create room for new, expansive fixtures, the couple chose to forsake a separate toilet enclosure or a tub. This left plenty of space to reconstruct a vintage room around a single element—the arched window and its scenic display.

Setting the mood for the new room and interacting with the natural illumination, cream-tone marble tiles create a light, tranquil foundation. The large tile continues on the wall, forming a wainscoting that maintains an uninterrupted look throughout the room. On the radiant heat floor, mosaic accent tiles provide delicate points of visual interest in a field of neutral tones.

Exploiting the newly created space, a dramatic dual-sink vanity establishes a refined, vintage environment. Crisp white paint on the cabinets brightens the marble's muted tones, and a rich cocoa-color marble countertop matches the title accents in the floor. With its Queen Anne-style feet, rounded cabinet doors, and undulating, curving lines, the vanity defines the room's vintage flavor. The countertop cabinet's frosted-glass windows, three tall, provide storage space without making the vanity visually overwhelming. Cabinets beneath the countertop and a freestanding armoire echo the rounded features and offer generous amounts of storage. "Now the bathroom functions very well and stays neat and tidy because everything has its place in the vanity and the linen cabinet," Valerie says.

Repeating the curved motif that complements the window, a rounded shower enclosure eases entry into the room. The clear enclosure guarantees an open, uninterrupted sight line. The glass is treated with a coating

AN UPWARD RISING ROMAN SHADE PRESERVES A VISTA EASILY VIEWED FROM THE NEW VANITY.

formulated to shed water and resist spotting. The roomy shower includes a handheld sprayer that is perfect for luxurious bathing and ideal for rinsing the glass enclosure. Extending the light color scheme, the shower is lined with the same marble tile and mosaic accents that appear on the floor.

While providing useful amenities, small details also add charm and personality. Towel hooks and rings provide visually pleasing convenience without occupying

Serving as the room's focal point, the broad dual-sink vanity provides ample storage with tall, glass-door towers above the countertop and broad, rounded cabinets below.

Pewter-finish cross-handle faucets and cocoa-color marble highlight the countertop, defining a rich, vintage sensibility.

The vanity is loaded with storage, including these cabinet towers that flank the mirrors.

A pullout basket in the freestanding wardrobe provides an easy-access hamper.

excessive wall space. Evoking bygone Edwardian style, vintage cross-handle faucets and rounded cabinet pulls display a refined, polished-pewter finish. To preserve the vista from the window, a Roman blind rises from the bottom rather than descending from the top.

Now, whether they're standing at the double sink or enjoying a hot shower, the Laskers are greeted with the glorious display from the window. With open space and carefully considered details, the room reclaims its heritage and is far more than a unique closet. "Even if our old bathroom had been perfect," Valerie reflects, consider-

ing the window and its panoramic scene, "gaining the view would have been enough for us to remodel."

A CURVED CLEAR-GLASS ENCLOSURE SURROUNDS THE NEW SHOWER, PERMITTING AN UNINTERRUPTED LINE OF SIGHT THROUGHOUT THE ROOM.

IN THE NEW, SPACIOUS SHOWER, CREAM MARBLE TILES MAINTAIN THE TRANQUIL COLOR TONES. A HANDHELD SPRAYER ADDS EXTRA CONVENIENCE.

FOUR-BY-FOUR-INCH TILES IN A SWIRLED PATTERN FORM A BACKSPLASH BEHIND THE SINKS. A SMALLER VERSION—THIS ONE 2×2-INCH—FRAMES THE MIRRORS.

CHECKERBOARD TILE TOPS THE TUB BACKSPLASH AND STAIR FRONTS —A SUBTLE ACCENT TO THE NEUTRAL PALETTE.

FROM THE SQUARE, CUSTOM-CONTOURED TUB, CAROLYN CAN REVEL IN THE VIEWS WHILE ENJOYING A STREAM OF WATER FROM THE GOOSENECK FAUCET, OR WATCH THE MARINERS ON THE LOW-VOLTAGE TV.

From the custom-contoured soaking tub perched high in her Mercer Island, Washington, master bath, Carolyn Feldsine has her pick of scenery: out the windows for a stunning view of Lake Washington, or toward the television for the Seattle Mariners baseball game. Whichever way she glances she's surrounded by elegance and comfort in a room that fulfills the demands of a busy work-a-day schedule or more relaxing pursuits.

The rectangular 18×11-foot room, designed by architect Mark Elster and interior designer Pamela Pearce for Carolyn and her husband, Phil, splits the toilet compartment into an enclosed room at the end of the space. Along one wall three columns separate two sinks; the vanity resembles a set of time-weathered antiques, and the dual sinks allow the couple to use the space without disturbing each other. The stylish built-ins boast three kinds of pulls and three finishes—glazed, crackled, and sealed— that hide any signs of daily wear and tear.

"We stayed away from shiny surfaces; instead there's tumbled stone, crackled finishes, and hammered-nickel

ELEVATED TUB TO FRAME VIEWS
INTERIOR WINDOWS TO CAST LIGHT
CHECKERBOARD MOSAIC ON STAIR FRONTS
COLUMNS THAT DOUBLE AS STORAGE

sinks that don't show fingerprints, scratches, or watermarks," Carolyn says.

The columns boost storage but don't take up floor and wall space. The central column does double duty, marking a change in ceiling height and holding mirror-doored medicine cabinets.

"We designed unfitted furniturelike pieces—with the suggestion of feet at the toe-kicks and recessed pierced-metal screen doors—that maximized the space," Elster says. "We included three columnar cabinets. With friezes defined by cove moldings around the top, the columns read as architectural elements instead of cabinets."

The ceiling vaults over the elevated square tub, allowing for an arched window that floods the space with sunshine and frames the lake view. Interior windows on either side of the tub pull light into the adjacent shower. A checkerboard mosaic repeated in the backsplash fronts the trio of stairs to the tub, which was custom-contoured to Carolyn's reclining body.

"Carolyn dressed in grubbies, and the tile setter put down heavy mesh, which she sat in," Elster says. "The mesh took her shape, then the tile setter applied the tile over the mesh form."

Throughout the room, Carolyn's love of rough natural textures emerges in weathered colors, ceramic tiles, sandy-hued hand-finished plaster walls, and the honed, tumbled, pillowed limestone used on floors, the tub surround and deck, and wainscoting. And while there's no chance of her catching a fly ball, Carolyn can revel in the Old World luxuries of her master bath.

"I can't think of anything to change. I wake up every day and think what a lucky woman I am," she says.

THE CENTRAL COLUMN HIDES STORAGE BEHIND THE MIRRORED MEDICINE CABINET. DUAL SINKS WITH A HAMMERED FINISH HIDE WATER SPOTS AND STAINS.

A CRACKLE FINISH ALLOWS FOR WEAR AND TEAR, WHILE ADDING TO THE OLD WORLD LOOK. MOLDING ACCENTS ON THE DRAWERS HIGHLIGHT THE VANITY'S PAIRS OF STEPPED-BACK PIERCED-METAL DOORS.

Grand Intimacy

Ample room greeted Liz and Larry Wolfe in their master bath. But what it had in space, the bath lacked in style. The cold, uninviting area dominated by huge, angular spaces lacked the charming French country facade of the Wolfes' house.

Liz and Larry asked interior designer Susan Geier to rework the 400-square-foot space into an elegant, approachable bathroom. Believing bigger is not always better, Geier made architectural changes to infuse the room with form and intimacy. She softened the room's hard edges by curving the perimeters of almost all the surfaces, including the steps, countertops, and bathtub alcove. Then she enclosed the different functional areas, such as the bathtub, shower, and toilet, to evoke a cozy, small room.

Reducing the walk-in shower size allowed Geier to add amenities such as a steam shower and multiple shower-

LASER-CUT MARBLE FORMS THE LEAF-PATTERN BORDER IN THE LIMESTONE FLOOR.

THE LUXURY OF STONE, WOOD, METAL, AND SILK CREATES AN INVITING RETREAT. CUSTOM FURNITURE-LIKE CABINETRY WITH INSET CARVED DOORS ANCHORS THE VANITY WALL AND CONTRIBUTES TO A FRENCH COUNTRY MOTIF.

THE TEXTURED MARBLE AND THE LIMESTONE BASKET-WEAVE BACKSPLASH CONTRAST WITH THE SMOOTH MARBLE COUNTERTOP AND PORCELAIN SINK.

The CRYSTAL-AND-BRASS CHANDELIER HANGING AT THE CENTER OF THE ROOM ADDS AMBIENT LIGHT AND ELEGANCE.

GLASS SHELVES IN THE TUB ALCOVE CREATE IDEAL DISPLAY SPACE FOR CANDLES AND BATH OILS.

heads. The leftover space provided room for a heated towel rack and built-in bench/hamper just outside the shower door.

Geier turned another wasted space into an asset by enclosing the original tub in a step-up arched alcove with wing walls and display shelves. "Architecturally we wanted to separate [the tub] a bit and add some interest there," she says.

The arch motif, which is repeated in the finely crafted wood vanity wall, helps establish the French country style. Aged pecan-finish cabinetry embellished with brass fixtures fills the vanity wall, contributing a refined air to the room and filling the large space. "We created elements that feel more like furniture than bathroom cabinets," Geier says. "We [also] incorporated different textures, materials, and levels of shine, from matte to glossy. It's more interesting if things don't match exactly but just blend together."

With that idea in mind, Geier designed an illuminated perfume cabinet to divide the two sinks and accompanying mirrors. Towels are stored in a stand-alone armoire copied from an antique.

Subtly varied colors and textures create interest but still retain a cohesive look. Six types of limestone and marble on the shower, tub surround, countertops, and flooring feature similar gold tones, so they enliven the bath without competing for attention.

Geier infused the bath with color by painting and glazing the gold walls to form a subdued, textured backdrop that complements the room's natural materials. The colors, combined with the crystal chandelier that throws diffused light over the room, envelop bathers in an ethereal glow.

"It's the combination of wood, stone, metal, and fabric that makes this bathroom rich," Geier says.

A FREESTANDING CUSTOM ARMOIRE STORES TOWELS. NEARBY A HEATED TOWEL RACK AND A BENCH THAT CONTAINS A HAMPER GREET BATHERS.

A LARGE, HIGH SHOWERHEAD CHANNELS WATER TO FLOW DOWNWARD RATHER THAN IN THE FACE.

COMPLETELY ENCLOSING THE SHOWER ALLOWED THE WOLFES TO INCLUDE A STEAM GENERATOR WITH SATIN-NICKEL CONTROLS.

Rarely do bathrooms receive the same treatment as other rooms in the house. But in Jennifer and Ralph Ehrenpreis' well-appointed master bath, known affectionately as a private living room, the roaring fire, wood paneling, and gleaming marble have all the trappings of a formal sitting room or den.

The room's plan focuses on a roomy raised corner tub, positioned for the perfect outside view from the couple's Bel Air, California, home. Wide ledges supply plenty of surface space for bath necessities. A seamless stretch of marble encases the tub deck and surround, continuing onto the floor and the fireplace wall and forming the vanity countertop.

"I like having the tub raised with the steps because when I get into the tub, there is a picture window right over it," Jennifer says. "I can see all over Los Angeles when I take a bath."

Just steps away, the fire warms the room on chilly days, a chair and ottoman create a comfy spot to sit and dry off, and an antique rug warms the sleek floor. Behind the fireplace, shelves hold Jennifer's favorite things. "I put everything—all my personal stuff—on the shelves, and that's why I call it my personal living room," she says. "I put my books in there, my CDs; all my little treasures are there."

Raised wood paneling forms the shelves behind the tub, continuing top to bottom on the walls and on the vanity's cabinet doors and drawers. The intricate moldings and detailed wood grain stand in calm contrast to the smooth gleam of marble.

On the vanity, an undermount sink maintains an unbroken surface. To hold clutter at bay, a wall panel near the sink opens to reveal a medicine cabinet stocked with lotions, oils, and perfumes.

Clear glass frames the marble floor and bench in the spacious steam shower, opposite the tub, to allow in

A TUB, FIREPLACE, CHAIR, OTTOMAN, AND ANTIQUE RUG FORM A MINI DEN NOOK, PERFECT FOR READING, BATHING, AND RELAXING.

An undermount sink allows for a seamless vanity view. Raised wood paneling for doors and drawers mimics the walls across the rest of the room.

scenic, light-filled views. "I like the fact that it's glass, so again, even when you're taking a shower you see the view," Jennifer says. "Even when the door is closed, you see everything."

A separate toilet compartment, styled to look like a walk-in closet, allows for privacy.

French doors lead to a rose- and container-filled balcony, with a treetop view of sprawling Los Angeles beyond. It's a fitting end to a stylish room, not just for bathing, but for living.

"I use my balcony every day," Jennifer says. "I sit out there and I have my cup of coffee."

NESTLED BEHIND A DOOR, A STORAGE COMPARTMENT TO THE LEFT OF THE VANITY KEEPS LOTIONS, OILS, AND PERFUMES HANDY, BUT HIDDEN.

NEXT TO THE GLASS-ENCLOSED SHOWER, A DOOR HIDES THE TOILET COMPARTMENT. A PLANT STAND AND BENCH OUTSIDE THE SHOWER DOOR COMPLETE THE FURNISHED-ROOM LOOK.

5 CONTEMPORARY FLAIR

Design a restorative spalike retreat with inspiration from the modern examples here. From sleek and stylish to colorful and fun, these rooms are anything but cold and sterile. Select state-of-the-art fixtures, such as streamlined spouts and a soothing soaking tub. Mix in lustrous surfaces—glass, maple, chrome, or shimmering mosaic tile. Flat-panel wood cabinetry maintains the simplicity of contemporary design. Surround showers with glass, or design open showers for a clean look. Include plenty of built-in, hidden storage to keep toiletries and grooming necessities out of sight. Eliminate the need for fussy window treatments with frosted glass or strategically positioned windows. Tranquil colors provide the finishing touches.

Contemporary Colors

Concrete, color, and contemporary style meld in this master bath, which underwent a bold transformation from bland 1980s decor to modern-art flair.

To celebrate their love of modern art, the homeowners bypassed the option of creating a period look for the interior of their 1907 Arts and Crafts home. "It was very vanilla—all neutral, standard materials," interior designer Lou Ann Bauer says. The couple craved something more cutting-edge. "They wanted a colorful, fun interior."

Accordingly, brilliant shades of lime and mango set the tone for the master bath's new look. Although the fixtures didn't move, unique treatments let each area stand out while harmonizing with the others. The dual-sink

WOOD, GLASS, CONCRETE, AND CHROME IN COLORFUL, SHAPELY RENDERINGS REFLECT THE OWNERS' LOVE OF CONTEMPORARY ART.

SYCAMORE CABINETRY AND A COLOR CONCRETE COUNTERTOP MAKE UP THE VANITY. THE INTEGRAL SINKS' ANGLED FRONTS FIT THE ROOM'S GEOMETRY AND INCREASE SINK VOLUME.

Bold, energizing colors
Frosted-glass windows
Colorful poured concrete floors

vanity, for example, is now a trapezoid, with figured sycamore cabinetry and a lime green concrete countertop. Selected drawers dyed mango and lime green enhance the sycamore's grain and add a splash to the room's color scheme. To top off the vanity area, round mirrors and shapely sconces offer fun and function.

Natural light from unadorned windows shines on the oval tub set in the corner, while the frosted-glass panes ensure privacy. Shades of lime green on the window frames and the tub's concrete surround echo the decor. Even the concrete floor and threshold match the green of the sinks.

A glass panel separates the tub from the equally open shower. Slablike 24×24-inch terrazzo tiles embedded with colorful glass chips form the shower walls. Two showerheads produce the effects of rain while a clever niche in the wall holds soap and shampoo.

The concept of a concrete floor takes on new life as two curvy slabs, one lime green and one mango, meet in the bath's middle like puzzle pieces. The poured concrete is as tough as ceramic tile, but without the disruption of grout lines.

Even the faucets, handles, and pulls in this bath have an artistic bent, most boasting unexpected shapes or colors. Bauer's take on the hardware applies to the room as a whole. "These are all functional pieces," she says, "but functional pieces can be fun shapes and colors."

Terrazzo wall tiles bring color and style to the walk-in shower.

The bath's contemporary design accentuates the sinuous curve, where the floor's mango and lime concrete slabs meet.

Plenty of light filtered through frosted-glass windows adds to the private spa impression of the tub area. The tub's corner-mounted controls are easily accessible, but not in the way.

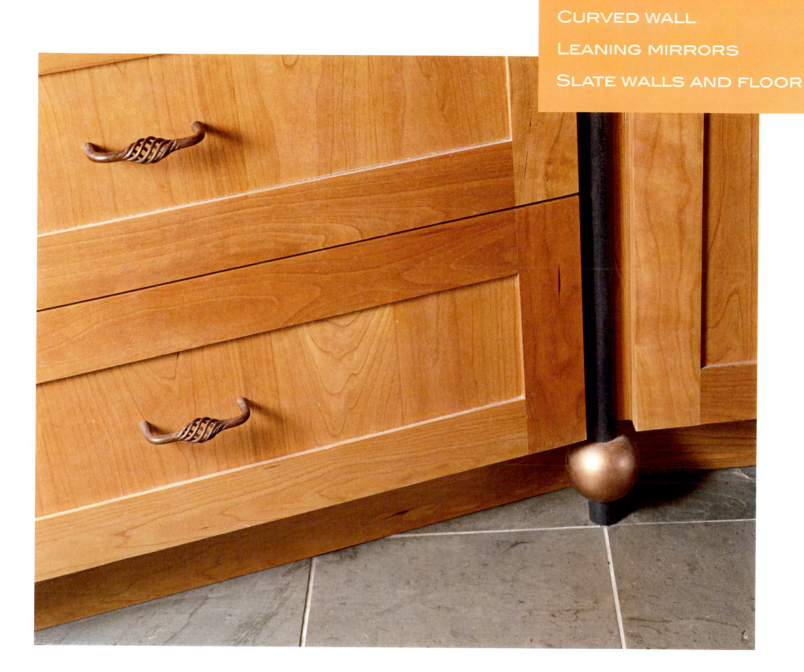

Jan and Scott deLuis wanted their loft to be both an architectural statement and a fully functional living space. Created from a former flour mill, the loft offered plenty of opportunity for creative living spaces. "They wanted to have something that was distinctive and memorable, but they also wanted it to be livable," architect Guy Thornton says. "They didn't want it to be a museum piece."

Inspired by the flour grinding process and the building's exterior, Thornton turned to stone as the primary element in the master bath. He envisioned the space as a sort of residential sculpture. "Think of a solid block of slate," he says, "and think of forming the bath out of that."

INSPIRED BY THE BUILDING'S EXTERIOR, GREEN SLATE AND SEA GREEN KIRKSTONE PROVIDE A DEEP, NATURAL TONE TO THE BATH. THE CURVING WALL OFFERS A FLOWING, SCULPTURAL ELEMENT.

METAL POSTS DETAILED WITH COPPER-TONE BALL FEET HELP DEFINE THE VANITY'S CRESCENT SHAPE.

131

Recalling the mill's original flour silos, the vanity wall curves, as do other rooms in the loft. Vermont green slate accented with white, diamond-shape tile covers the walls and floor, creating the sense of a stone enclosure. Dark slabs of kirkstone—a sea green volcanic rock—form the countertops and add to the grandeur.

While stone adds a clean formality to the space, warm cherry cabinets along with creative lighting counter the darker tones. Recessed ceiling lights and a bare-bulb wall fixture highlight the various textures and colors.

Since the room lacks a window to the outside, mirrors create an intriguing play of light. Along the curved wall, mirrors lean away from the wall, distributing light throughout the space. A floor-to-ceiling mirrored wall broadly reflects the entire room and divides the toilet compartment and an open shower. Polished, reflective metal, such as chrome fixtures and burnished, copper-tone cabinet details, continue the theme of natural material.

Combining stone, wood, light, and other elements creates a dynamic, natural blend. The interplay of light and curving architecture adds a sense of movement to a space that is rich and heavy in tone. Nestled in the heart of an urban center, this room creates an organic, sculptural oasis that remains true to its working heritage. Establishing a balance between art and function, this bath is a finely crafted live-in sculpture garden, perfect for visionary, yet practical, city dwellers.

A CEILING-MOUNTED RAIN-STYLE SHOWERHEAD HIGH-LIGHTS THE OPEN SHOWER. A MIRRORED WALL SEPARATING THE TOILET COMPARTMENT PROVIDES A BROAD FIELD OF REFLECTED LIGHT.

BASIC INSTINCTS

For architect Pat Killen, simplicity leads to the most elegant results. So when he grappled with the constrained master bath of this oceanfront home, he decided to reduce the space to its most basic elements, creating a transcendent room along the way.

The constricted space offered creative challenges. Despite the home's scenic ocean views, the bathroom had limited space for windows due to the building's roofline. Undaunted, Killen drew inspiration from the home's contemporary architecture, using clean lines and broad combinations of natural material to establish quality. "We decided to select materials that stand the test of time," Killen says.

White and blue expanses on the walls are grounded by earthy, blue-veined limestone on the floors, countertops, and tub. The vanity features maple and cherry cabinets, which balance the cooler textures with a warm, organic base. To create a greater sense of spaciousness, a broad mirror occupies almost the entire vanity wall, reflecting color and light throughout the area.

The tub solidly anchors one wall, and the shower is enclosed at the end of an abbreviated hallway. Besides

SLENDER, WALL-MOUNTED FAUCETS AND NARROW, BLUE LIGHT SCONCES INSTILL ELEGANT UTILITY WITHOUT DISRUPTING THE MIRROR'S REFLECTION.

PAIRED WITH A RECTANGULAR AWNING WINDOW, A SKYLIGHT IN THE GROTTOLIKE SHOWER CREATES A CASCADING LIGHT EFFECT.

BESIDES PROVIDING NEEDED STORAGE, THE CLOSET ALSO USES A FULL-LENGTH MIRROR TO VISUALLY ENLARGE THE SPACE.

creating the impression that the room is larger, the short corridor also makes the shower seem more private and tucked away, like a small grotto. "It gives you that kind of wraparound effect," Killen notes. "It really cradles you."

The inspired remedy for the minimal windows is a skylight running almost the entire length of the ceiling. Partnered with rectangular awning windows, the skylight compensates for the lack of an outdoor view and provides a continuous field of natural illumination. In the shower another long skylight separates the ceiling and wall. That allows, as Killen observes, "the skylight to be the strong element in the area and that blue wall to really feel like it's just falling, cascading underneath it as a second feature."

With a spare, modern sensibility the room combines color, mirrors, and texture to create a harmonious, timeless blend. Bold, Dresden blue tile on two walls and in the shower draws out the delicate indigo veins in the marble. Unornamented wood cabinets, closet frame, and shelving soften the bold colors and preserve a clean, uncluttered space. "The underlying motivation," Killen says, "was to try and make it elegant, and yet very simple."

Clean, clear design choices ultimately lead this room to practical and elegant results.

WITH LITTLE ROOM FOR WINDOWS, A BROAD, CEILING-LENGTH SKYLIGHT PROVIDES A WIDE FIELD OF ILLUMINATION.

AN ABBREVIATED CORRIDOR TO THE SHOWER MAKES THE ROOM SEEM LARGER AND ADDS PRIVACY.

UNADORNED DRAWERS AND CABINETS MAINTAIN A CLEAN, SLEEK APPEARANCE.

For a bath to exude simplicity and serenity, architects Jerrold E. Lomax and Zoltan E. Pali contend less is more. "You have a sense of freedom when you can move easily through a space," Pali says, "and there are no unnecessary visual obstructions." The benefits of their philosophy transcend aesthetics. "Minimalism in design is very calming," Lomax says. "Society is chaotic, so we try to simplify."

It's this philosophy that Chris and Sally Nicol Benjamin envisioned for their master bathroom. But though they wanted simplicity and serenity, the couple wasn't about to sacrifice luxury or space.

"They wanted something that would be two baths in one," Lomax says, "each having their own semiprivate areas for getting ready in the morning while still keeping the bathroom as one large open space they could share."

To meet the Benjamins' needs without carving the 11×18-foot area into a warren of compartments, Pali and Lomax planned the room as two zones: one for bathing and relaxing, and another for dual grooming. Both zones offer the well-appointed luxuries the Benjamins yearned for, including a Japanese soaking tub, a large dual-head shower, and a walk-in sauna.

At one end of the room a trio of extra-large windows high on the wall allows light to shine, but retains privacy. The bathing zone forms beneath the windows, where the deep tub with a granite bench, a large open shower, and the door to the sauna line up along the wall. A suspended glass partition prevents shower water from spraying onto the floor beyond, but allows light and views to flow freely throughout the bathroom.

The Benjamins love the convenience of the configuration. "We can use the sauna, then step under the shower and cool off. It's wonderful," Chris says. When the couple use their Japanese tub in its traditional manner, they begin with a long, relaxing soak in extra-hot water. A granite bench and handheld showerhead between the tub and shower provide a convenient niche for soaping and rinsing off before another dip in the tub. Once the ritual is complete, warmed towels on the heated towel racks at the end of the vanity await the relaxed bather.

The architects "floated" the large walnut-veneer vanity in the center of the room to provide separate grooming areas. "The vanity cabinet doesn't rest on the floor," Pali explains. "Instead, it is supported by two steel posts far underneath and out of sight. It creates the feeling that it is floating."

To further that effect, back-to-back mirrors hang from the ceiling above the vanity. The bottom of the mirrors

SEPARATE FUNCTIONAL AREAS
SPA-STYLE AMENITIES
"FLOATING" MIRRORS
HEATED TOWEL RACKS

hovers several inches above the granite slab countertop, offering privacy without hindering communication between the Benjamins when they're at their respective grooming stations on opposing sides of the mirror.

Between the end of the vanity and the wall, back-to-back toilet compartments are tucked into a slice of space. Walnut veneer partitions provide medicine cabinets for the sinks and storage niches for the toilet compartments.

DUAL SHOWERHEADS EXTENDING FROM THE CEILING COVER THE OVERSIZE BATHING AREA AND TWO BATHERS. THE ATTACHED SAUNA OFFERS EVEN MORE SPALIKE RELAXATION.

THE STATIONARY GLASS WALL SUSPENDED BY STAINLESS STEEL HOLDERS OPENS AT BOTH ENDS FOR ACCESS TO THE BATHING AREA.

Light gray porcelain tiles with a matte finish create slip-resistant flooring throughout the bath. In keeping with the goal of simplicity, the 12×12-inch tiles restrict grout lines to a minimum. Smaller, slip-resistant tiles make a practical choice for the shower and tub area.

Teamed with soft white walls, the elements come together for a look that's easy on the eye, calming for the spirit, and luxurious to the body.

PLACING THE TUB AND SHOWER BENEATH A BANK OF WINDOWS ALLOWS DIRECT VENTILATION OF STEAM AND CONFINES WET AREAS AT ONE END OF THE ROOM. A LEDGE THAT SPANS THE FULL LENGTH OF THE TUB AND SHOWER AREA PROVIDES A PERCH FOR BATHING ACCOUTREMENTS.

THE CUSTOM-BUILT SOAKING TUB FEATURES ANGLED ENDS FOR COMFORT.

is suspended from the wall. "It's an exotic wood with a subtle visual texture," Philipp says. "Lifting the vanity off the floor creates the illusion of more space."

In the end, though, it's not the illusion of the scene but the reality outside the windows that draws Jack. "I love to see the shoreline, the ocean, and the waves," he says.

A LARGE CENTRAL SKYLIGHT AND WIDE RECTANGULAR WINDOWS DRAW SUNLIGHT INTO THE MASTER BATH.

THE WINDOW ABOVE THE TUB—WHICH WRAPS AROUND THE CORNER—ALLOWS BREEZES AND SUNLIGHT TO ENTER WITHOUT SACRIFICING PRIVACY.

THE LARGE CURVED SHOWER INCLUDES A FIXED SHOWERHEAD, AS WELL AS A CONVENIENT HANDHELD ONE FOR FLEXIBILITY AND EASIER RINSING OF WALLS.

A third-floor addition to their oceanside home gave Jack and Connie Mahoney a master suite that echoes the beach views it offers.

A dramatic framework of interlocking wood beams and a skylight punctuates the high ceiling above the 12×10-foot bath. Wide rectangular windows allow ocean breezes and more light to drift in without sacrificing privacy.

This solid visual connection to the outdoors inspired architect Michael Lee and interior designer Susan Philipp to allow nature to influence their choices for materials. "The views are extraordinary," Lee says, "and we wanted to bring that same serenity and calmness indoors."

Jerusalem Gold marble slabs—cut into a variety of rectangular sizes—wrap the room's walls like a golden beach. To echo the translucency of water, hand-cut glass mosaic tiles cover the floor, and laminated-glass privacy panels shield the toilet area and curving shower from view. "When you look down at the glass tiles," Jack says, "you see this shimmering effect that makes you feel like you are walking on water."

For yet another floating effect, a simply styled vanity made of anigre veneer topped with Oasis Yellow marble

Thinking outside the box provided a fresh take in the design of Melissa and Todor Fay's master bath—with shapely results.

Challenging long-held notions of what a bath should be, Melissa and Todor chose to forgo the typical bathroom arrangement by taking the toilet out of the equation. Architect Lane Williams created a separate, self-contained powder room elsewhere in the master suite to house the toilet.

Though unconventional, moving the toilet opened up space in the master bath for three related functions—bathing, grooming, and dressing. "When you think about it, the toilet doesn't have to be in the same space," Williams says. "Bathing and dressing can be more easily combined in one space if you don't have to work around a toilet."

The bath's trapezoid-shape dressing area consists of a maple vanity and matching chests of drawers on one side of the room. Generous closets and drawers fill the opposite wall. Such an arrangement simplifies and accelerates getting ready for work.

"We absolutely love the logic of it," Melissa says. "Showering, brushing our teeth, combing our hair, and dressing all in one area makes so much sense."

Beyond the dressing area a curved exterior wall embraces the bathing room. The two areas combine to occupy the second floor of a tower set apart from the lakeside home's main structure. "The house sits on a steep site overlooking a lake, and there's a view of the water from a corner window," Williams says. "The boat shape seemed like an appropriate reference, as well as a way to keep sharp corners out of the room."

A sunken claw-foot tub set into a boat-shape surround advances the contoured theme. "I love to read in the tub," Melissa says, "and unlike newer models this older style is deeper and has a slope that you can recline against comfortably. It's also nice to just sit there and gaze out through the window to the lake."

ONE-INCH-THICK CLEAR GLASS TOPS THE NATURAL-FINISH MAPLE VANITY. BUILT-IN CHESTS OF DRAWERS STAND ON EACH SIDE. ON THE OPPOSITE WALL TRANSLUCENT GLASS ON THE CLOSET'S SLIDING DOORS CONCEALS THE CONTENTS.

Although the tub is spacious enough to accommodate the couple's two young sons, Melissa says the boys prefer the open shower at the opposite end of the room. "They like to take their dump trucks in there and play and get clean at the same time. We just aim the two showerheads in two directions and hope that one will hit them," she says. The absence of an enclosure of any kind makes access to the shower easy for children and adults alike. "Besides," Melissa says, "I didn't want any glass shower doors to have to clean."

The honed finish of the limestone floor tile in both rooms provides traction and retains a slight reflective

quality. Variations in tile patterns, sizes, and shapes add visual interest and texture, especially in the absence of strong colors. The dressing area features 12-inch squares; tiles of the same size were cut into 3-inch squares for the bathing-area floor and tub surround.

The strong geometric shapes of both spaces appeal to the Fays' artistic sensibilities. "We didn't want a one-note house where every room is a square or a rectangle," Melissa says. "We had a strong desire to see the house as a sculpture. It's a very contemporary bath, but the shapes of the spaces and the texture and tone of the materials make it very warm and inviting."

An Elegant Workhorse

When done well, a bathroom provides both function and fashion, balancing practicality and looks. The surfaces and fixtures in Leslie and Mark Werksman's master bath work double duty to create an elegant, efficient space.

The Werksmans turned to architect Patrick Killen and interior designer Kelly Teddy for a retreat that would help the working couple get going in the morning, but reward them with a soothing experience for lingering stays. Bathing options abound, starting with a deep

CONTEMPORARY FIXTURES FLOW INTO THE LARGE TUB SURROUNDED BY A CHECKERBOARD OF LIMESTONE TILE. BEHIND THE GLASS WALLS OF THE SHOWER, GLEAMING BLACK CERAMIC TILE REFLECTS LIGHT FROM A WINDOW CUTOUT.

CONCRETE SINKS SIT ABOVE THE COUNTERTOP; CONTEMPORARY FAUCETS SPARKLE IN THE MIRROR.

soaking tub set into a limestone tile surround. The team chose tile in two neutral shades, placing it in a checkerboard pattern on the deck as well as the floor.

Adjacent to the tub is a copious glass-enclosed shower. Limestone tile forms the shower floor too, but the back wall breaks from the warm palette with a cool gleaming surface of black ceramic squares. Between the shower and wall, a drying-off nook unites each material in the room—glass, ceramic tile, limestone, and maple. Hooks hold towels; below the sitting bench are cabinets for storage.

Across from the tub and shower wall, separate grooming areas for the couple divide a long vanity. In its center is a makeup station at sit-down height. Concrete sinks "float" partially above the countertop; their matte finish reflects in the gleam of the contemporary chrome faucets and mirrored glass wall. A marble mosaic countertop crowns the light, neutral finish of the bird's-eye maple

THE SEAMLESS GRID OF DOORS AND DRAWERS ON THE VANITY BREAKS AT THE HANDCRAFTED MOSAIC COUNTERTOP. A SIT-DOWN COSMETIC COUNTER AND A WALL OF MIRRORS MAKE THE SERENE SPOT A PRACTICAL SETUP.

THE WOOD GRAIN IN THE CABINETS AND VANITY ECHOES THE ROUND PIECES IN THE MOSAIC, HANDCRAFTED AND INFUSED WITH FLECKS OF ORANGE, BLUE, AND YELLOW.

cabinetry. Irregularly shaped squares and circles, dashed with tiny bits of orange and blue, liven up the mosaic which was hand-assembled onto mesh sheets and "rolled over" at the countertop's edge. The handcrafted look is a warm counterpoint to the room's otherwise seamless surfaces.

Opposite the vanity a grid of floor-to-ceiling maple doors hides large storage compartments for towels, bed linens, and travel gear. The couple opted for push-open latches in lieu of hardware to maintain the clean look. The room comes full circle with the floor-to-ceiling mirror that connects the tall bank of cabinetry with the vanity. It's practical as a viewing area, and gives the illusion of more space in the modest 17×12-foot room.

If sophisticated were practical, the Werksmans' bathroom fits the bill, a serene mix designed for ease, durability, and elegance.

INSET INTO A SMALL NICHE, A BENCH UNITES THE ROOM'S MATERIALS AND ADDS A PRACTICAL DRYING-OFF SPACE OUTSIDE THE SHOWER.

PUSH-OPEN LATCHES MAINTAIN A SEAMLESS SURFACE ON THE CABINETS, WHERE TOWELS, BED LINENS, AND TRAVEL GEAR ARE STORED.

PICTURE PERFECT

Designer Jean Verbridge faced an intriguing challenge when designing this master bathroom in a seaside Boston-area home—complementing rather than competing with the stunning views of the lush, formal gardens and ocean just beyond.

Verbridge crafted a clean, contemporary look for the space that perfectly frames nature's picture beyond the room. The bath focuses on two themes: smooth, simple lines and clean, pure white. "Everything in the room is simple, round, clean, and pure," Verbridge says.

She started with a Philippe Starck oval tub the homeowner had chosen. "It's pure geometry," Verbridge says of the freestanding tub. Within the angled six-sided room, the tub was the first element to offer softness. Smooth lines in the bath continue with perfectly round white basin sinks that sit atop white granite countertops. "It's the whitest granite we could find," Verbridge says. "It looks perfectly clean."

Tone-on-tone whites continue with white plaster walls. Applied white trim moldings around the marble steam shower, ceiling, and floor lend texture and a slight traditional touch to the otherwise contemporary space. Radiant heat warms French vanilla-color marble floors.

Even the halogen lighting is consistent with the design theme. "It's pure-white light," Verbridge says. "It's good light for putting on makeup or shaving. It's also a relaxing light."

Only the sandblasted glass doors to the shower and toilet and the aqua-color rug depart from the white. Both recall the water from the nearby ocean.

However, the clean, white room does not feel or look cold. A gas fireplace between the sink and shower offers physical as well as visual warmth. A built-in seat with a terry cloth cushion is a convenient spot to curl up in front of the fire or dry off after a relaxing soak. Floor-length translucent draperies soften the edges of the bay window

LUXURIES ABOUND IN THIS SPARE SPACE. A FIRE-PLACE, TERRY-COVERED BENCH, AND RADIANT HEAT FLOORS ALL PROVIDE WARMTH AND COMFORT.

and cut the glare from the ocean. "You can close them, but you still get a feel for the outdoor space beyond," Verbridge says.

The white room and large picture window topped with a semicircular transom had unexpected benefits as well: The white marble and granite surfaces glow when the room is bathed in moonlight. "The way the white reflects the moonlight was totally unplanned," Verbridge says. "That's where nature is better than we are." And that was the intention of the room all along—to frame nature at its best.

VIEWS OF THE FORMAL GARDEN AND OCEAN INSPIRED THE CLEAN, SIMPLE LINES OF THIS BATH.

SANDBLASTED-GLASS DOORS OFFER PRIVACY FOR THE TOILET AND SHOWER COMPARTMENTS, BUT ALLOW NATURAL LIGHT TO FILTER THROUGH.

UNCLUTTERED CALM

THE DISTINCTIVE EDGE OF THE SINK RUNS UP A SLOPE TO MEET THE SHINY, CONTEMPORARY FAUCETS. A WIDE LEDGE ALLOWS PLENTY OF ROOM FOR A BURST OF COLORFUL FLOWERS.

DUAL MIRRORS HANG IN FRONT OF A PANE OF FROSTED GLASS THAT DIVIDES THE DINING ROOM FROM THE BATHROOM. WHITE SINKS AND LIGHT-FINISH BAMBOO FLOORING BOUNCE LIGHT FROM SURFACE TO SURFACE.

With a mix of essential ingredients and a limited number of finishes, interior designer and homeowner Katy Boone created a master bath that is opened up to light and organized for function. "I wanted it to be very neutral and contemporary, and it ended up with an Asian feel," Katy says of her peaceful bathing retreat.

Katy kept space divisions at a minimum and visible clutter at bay by carefully thinking through the bathroom's requirements. A nearby closet provides space for toiletries, so the room needed little cabinetry. Shower

OPEN SHOWER WITH BENCH FOR STORAGE
CONTINUOUS TILE FROM TUB TO SINK
HANGING BEVELED-EDGE MIRRORS
FROSTED GLASS TO MAXIMIZE LIGHT

seating and storage came from an Asian-style teak bench purchased at an outdoor furniture store. A contemporary beech-and-chrome stool turned the countertop into a handy dressing table. "My father was an architect who once lived in Japan—this bath has the neat, minimal, soothing look of Japanese homes that I saw pictures of when I was a child," Katy says.

Paramount to the design was light: Katy maximized it by keeping materials bright and reflective. Twin beveled vanity mirrors hang from a metal rod, suspended in front of a pane of frosted glass that separates the bathroom from high windows in the adjacent two-story dining room. Frosted glass encloses the toilet, and the bottom half of the room's single exterior window also was frosted for privacy. Large gray tiles pave the floor of the open shower. "When you're in the open shower, there's natural light dancing all around you," Katy says. "You never feel like you're trapped in a box."

Pretty 1-inch tiles in varying shades of gray and blue pave the walls, tub enclosure, and vanity countertop. The generous deck and deep ledges of the tub surround supply the perfect resting space for soaps and sponges. The uninterrupted flow of tile from bath to counter maintains a minimalist and soothing aesthetic. White sinks flash against the tile; sparkling single-pull fixtures accent the sinks' upward floating bowl edge.

A wide doorway into the adjacent master bedroom directs more light into the bath. "The mirrors hanging on that partition reflect light coming in through windows, situated directly opposite them in my bedroom," Katy says.

Just a few simple materials, mixed with minimal curves and angles, sculpt a room filled with Zenlike tranquility. "It's definitely a space that's soothing in its simplicity," Katy says.

DEEP LEDGES AROUND THE TUB PROVIDE STORAGE SPACE. AN ADJACENT OPEN SHOWER FEATURES A FLOOR OF LARGER BLUE-GRAY TILES.

DOUBLE DELIGHT

Style needed to coalesce with shared convenience for these homeowners. Since both prepare for their day at the same time, they wanted to share space efficiently without sacrificing elegance.

To solve their congested schedule, the new bathroom utilizes a double-sided vanity that divides the room. Each side provides a sink, toilet, and shower, allowing the couple to share the room without disrupting their individual routines.

The structural design is intended to facilitate the homeowners' busy lifestyles, while the decor establishes serenity. One side features a large whirlpool bath with a marble enclosure. Honey-tone maple forms sleek, clean-lined vanities and cabinets. As an intriguing detail the wood is also used as a floor element next to the bath. Soothing, muted Botticino marble on the walls and countertops provides a stately, earthen feel to complement the wood fixtures.

Broad, wall-length picture windows allow in sunlight, making the outdoor view a natural, green background for the entire room. Most dramatically, a striking, translucent skylight arches overhead, bathing the entire space in natural illumination. Even as each person prepares for the day, the room allows the homeowners to comfortably share their space, bound by a tranquil arch of golden-hued light.

A VAULTED, ARCHING SKYLIGHT ILLUMINATES AND ENHANCES THE GOLDEN COLOR SCHEME.

THE MARBLE TUB ENCLOSURE EXTENDS INTO ONE OF THE INDIVIDUAL SHOWERS, FORMING A LUXURIOUS BENCH.

COUNTER SPACE AND AMPLE CABINET STORAGE FOR TWO ACTIVE INDIVIDUALS COME FROM THE DOUBLE-SIDED VANITY.

SCULPTURAL SHOWPIECE

Bathrooms and works of art typically have little in common. That is not the case with Stephen and Tami Logsdon's master bath designed by architect Paul D. Mankins.

"I had the idea to make something with an abstract object in the middle of the room instead of having a series of fixtures that line the walls," Mankins says. His creation is a work of art.

A simple spout emerges from a large mirror suspended from a sheet of glass mounted above a polished granite vanity in the center of the room. The sculptural element can be viewed from the entire room. Plumbing for the bath hides inside steel casings that run from floor to ceiling, allowing the vanity as well as the bathtub and shower to be centered in the room.

The contemporary bath presents a drastic change from the once-claustrophobic bathroom in the Logsdons' Craftsman-style cottage. Besides being cramped, the former bath didn't fit the couple's clean, minimalist tastes. While most of the new space distinctly departs from the old, the bath has two elements true to the home's original style: The hardwood floors and the window casings and trim replicate those in the rest of the home.

The result is a unique transformation. "It's like having a modern piece of sculpture in the middle of a 1920s house," Mankins says. "It's not your conventional bathroom."

STEEL CASINGS CONCEAL PLUMBING AND ALLOW FIXTURES TO EMERGE DRAMATICALLY FROM GLASS AND MIRRORED WALLS AT THE CENTER OF THE ROOM.

GLASS WALLS DEFINE AN OPEN SHOWER BETWEEN THE TUB AND VANITY. THE ENTIRE AREA RESTS ON A GRANITE PLATFORM.

PART ART, PART FUNCTION, A STEEL BASIN SITS ON A POLISHED GRANITE VANITY.

Dual Identity

Designed to tightly fit the double vanity, a sliding, frosted-glass divider creates both a small powder room for guests and a master bath that connects to the master bedroom.

Swiveling hinged shelves provide an elegantly simple solution to storage and create the sense of a walk-in closet.

Despite the close quarters of their 1948 Cape Cod-style cottage, Leanne and Billiam Coronel were intent on having a master bath without disturbing their home's balanced style. Confronted with tight spaces they recognized that a new master bath would also have to serve as a visitor's powder room.

The approach involved a little expansive thinking and a lot of creativity. By taking space from an old closet area and adding an entryway into the master bedroom, the small original bathroom was transformed to serve two

MARTINEZ VALERO

A BRIEF WALL PRODUCES A SMALL, PRIVATE TOILET ENCLOSURE AND SUPPORTS THE GLASS DIVIDER THAT SLIDES OUT TO CREATE A DOUBLE-USE ROOM.

A GLASS SHOWER WALL MAINTAINS OPENNESS AND ALLOWS NATURAL LIGHT TO ENTER THE ENTIRE ROOM FROM A LONG EYE-LEVEL WINDOW.

THE WARM, NATURAL TONE OF THE CHERRY DOORS CREATES A BLENDED TRANSITION FROM THE BATH TO THE LIVING ROOM'S DARKER WOOD FEATURES.

ELEVATED SINK BASINS AND SLEEK WALL-MOUNTED FAUCETS INTRODUCE A SENSE OF OPENNESS AND CLEAR, UNCLUTTERED SPACE.

roles. In the newly remodeled space an innovative frosted-glass divider slides across the room and mounts onto a double vanity. This gliding wall allows the homeowners to create one large bathroom or two separate spaces with different identities. One space is a convenient powder room, with a vanity and toilet, that connects to the living room. The second space is a master bath featuring half of the vanity, a tub and shower combination, and the new entrance into the master bedroom.

While creative choices may define the room's purpose, the space doesn't sacrifice style to meet functional needs. A clean-lined simplicity dominates the room's ambience, creating a sense of refreshing openness. The vanity features wall-mounted faucets to maintain a clear, spacious countertop area. In harmony with white vessel sink basins, the cabinets are raised slightly from the floor, producing a light, elevated appearance. Natural light illuminates the entire space through a long, eye-level

window in the shower, making the space feel bright and inviting even when the glass divider is closed.

Natural materials maintain serenity and blend the room with the rest of the house. Honey-color maple cabinets and limestone tile provide warm textures, while preserving a light sensibility in a small space. A cherry door offsets the dark woods of the living room, and the maple cabinets partner with new cabinetry in the master bedroom. Creating the sense of a walk-in closet, the passage between the bedroom and the bath features two columnlike storage towers that swivel outward to expose even more space for hanging clothes.

Without dramatically remodeling their charming, if tiny, home, the Coronels have a convenient powder room for visitors and a soothing, resplendent master bath. Even when confronted with a limited area, this bath proves that a little innovation can make more luxury with less space.

6 VINTAGE COMFORT

Provide an invitation for your own comfortable relaxation right at home with a vintage bath. No need for fuss or formality here. Just surround yourself with comfortable style, and amenities that will help soothe and allow you to relax. A large, deep claw-foot tub sets the stage for a vintage look and provides the ideal spot to soothe aching muscles. Create a sitting area with a comfortable chair and a small side table to hold bath amenities, reading materials, and a cup of tea. The chair doesn't need to be fancy. Try a flea market find slipcovered with terry cloth for an easy, relaxed look. Rather than standard built-in cabinetry, utilize timeworn free-standing furniture pieces with character.

Luck, Fate, and Charm

The heart of Cathy and Kirt Kaempfer's 1920s bungalow sits squarely in the Victorian era, but the home's bathroom is definitively from a different time period. When major plumbing problems developed shortly after they moved in, the couple turned the headache to their advantage, transforming a nondescript space into a room connected squarely with their home's past.

Similar Victorian homes fill the Kaempfer's historic neighborhood. A remodel needed to be sensitive to the setting. The result—full of vintage charm—came together with a little luck, careful planning, and good design.

The new-looking whirlpool tub was the first to go. In the midst of the room's gutting, the woman who bought the Kaempfers' previous home called to say she was getting rid of the old-fashioned tub Cathy loved. Its platform base and gentle curves radiate vintage charm. A pair of home improvement center pedestal sinks complete the period plumbing.

Cathy scoured flea markets for freestanding unmatched fixtures and finishes that add charm. A white chandelier and baker's rack for storage pair with a metal chair. Dual secondhand-store mirrors hang above the sinks, and a basket from a discount retailer holds towels. A flowing shower curtain was fashioned from bed linens; its paisley pattern picks up the vibrant red painted to wainscot height and continues the master bedroom's color scheme. The couple splurged on 8×8-inch Italian tiles. In three colors and patterns, their faded hue and imperfect edges add the perfect vintage touch.

The flavor of new and old is a perfect fit for the room's charm. "It's old-fashioned and it's simple," Cathy says.

THE LOVELY, IMPERFECT EDGES OF ITALIAN TILES WERE THE COUPLE'S BIG SPLURGE. THREE COLORS AND THREE PATTERNS FINISH OFF THE VINTAGE STYLE.

FASHIONED FROM BED LINENS, THE PAISLEY SHOWER CURTAIN FLOWS AROUND THE TUB.

DUAL PEDESTAL SINKS AND SECONDHAND-STORE MIRRORS STAND OUT IN WHITE. RED WAS PAINTED TO WAINSCOT HEIGHT, TOPPED BY A CHAIR RAIL. THE TUB, RESCUED FROM THE COUPLE'S FORMER HOME, MATCHES THE IRON SCROLLWORK ON THE BAKER'S RACK. BASKETS ADD BEAUTY AND STORAGE.

Shower curtain from pretty bed linens

Dual pedestal sinks

Found chandelier and baker's rack

Italian tiles

VINTAGE REVISITED

When Phil Wessels and Jana Stryker purchased a large, tree-filled lot for their family, they were more enamored of the California redwoods than the accompanying cottage. While the space and amenities were less than suitable, the new owners wanted to redefine the quaint 1920s residence by blending traditional cottage charm with their love of the surrounding timber.

As architect Barbara Chambers built a new residence, Jana was drawn to the sophistication of British-inspired details. "When we were building, we didn't want it to look new," Jana says. "I wanted it to look good 10 years from now, to look classic."

Showcasing this collaboration of timeless design with contemporary considerations, the remodeled master bath exhibits a crisp vintage style. The room features high, vaulted ceilings formed by the lines of the roof. Suggesting the comforting attic rooms often found in old homes, this dormer effect creates a classic sense of tucked-away privacy without the loss of useful space.

Providing the room's visual foundation and mimicking the effect of an area rug, marble tiles interlace in a delicate basket-weave design surrounded by a border. Inspired by the surrounding natural beauty, the floor's pale-green marble partners with muted-green walls in a refreshing combination.

White beaded-board wainscoting grounds the room in a clean, inviting sense of tradition. Beaded-board paired with white marble continues around the tub enclosure, where a bridge faucet and telephone-handle shower reiterates the English influence. Contributing to the evocation of bygone style, shuttered double-hung windows coordinate with wide base moldings and detailed door cornices. "All the details come from historic elements," Chambers says. "[For a room like this] you take old, familiar references and you make them more contemporary, a little cleaner."

Seeking to keep the space simple, two porcelain sinks with gooseneck faucets remain uncluttered because of deep, custom-made cabinets. Larger storage space is found in twin walk-in closets behind the sink wall. A stately, unobtrusive shower stall and a discreet, enclosed toilet compartment help maintain a clear, open space that holds attention on the family's preferred decorative element—the view from the windows. "I love taking a bath," Jana says. "I can open up the windows and look out at the trees."

CRISP, UNCLUTTERED SINKS WITH POLISHED GOOSENECK FAUCETS ESTABLISH THE ATMOSPHERE OF VINTAGE SIMPLICITY, WHILE DEEP, CUSTOM-MADE CABINETS OFFER HIDDEN STORAGE.

FEATURING A PALE GREEN HUE, A MARBLE BASKETWEAVE PATTERN PAIRED WITH A BANDED BORDER PROVIDES AN INTRICATE FOUNDATION TO THE ROOM.

A MODERN WHIRLPOOL TUB, FEATURING A CLASSIC, ENGLISH-STYLE HAND SPRAYER, HELPS FRAME THE WINDOW VIEW.

Laundry in the Loo

BLACK AND WHITE MARBLE TILES FORM A BASKET-WEAVE DESIGN ON THE FLOOR. THE SAME TILES PUNCTUATE THE 3×6-INCH WHITE SUBWAY TILES ON THE WALL.

FOR MORE VINTAGE STYLING, SUBWAY TILES FRAME THE RECESSED MEDICINE CABINET ABOVE THE SINK. BECAUSE SPACE IS TIGHT, THE POLISHED CHROME FRAME OF THE SINK BASE INCLUDES BARS FOR HOLDING GUEST TOWELS.

No one really looks forward to doing laundry, but Valerie Lasker particularly disliked the task. "I actually dreaded doing laundry," she says. "I was forever running up and down the stairs; it was too much work."

Valerie, an interior designer, decided to move her laundry facility from the basement to the second floor of her two-story San Francisco home. Her idea combined the guest bath with an unused furnace chase and part of the old master bath. The reconfigured space gained enough room for a washer, dryer, and storage, as well as a standard-size bathtub-shower combination, toilet, and sink.

Valerie chose vintage-style elements for a look befitting the old house. "We wanted a classically styled, elegant bathroom that was in keeping with the house's Edwardian heritage," she says.

To make the room seem more spacious, Valerie chose reflective finishes and white surfaces punctuated with black, such as the marble tile basket-weave pattern on the floor. A band of the same black and white tile also offsets the walls' white subway tiles.

Even the sink plays up the look. "I chose a small sink

SINK WITH POLISHED CHROME BASE
TIMELESS BLACK AND WHITE COMBO
CONCEALED LAUNDRY AREA

on chrome legs so it doesn't appear bulky," she says. "Plus, I just loved the vintage look."

Opposite the sink area a wall of cabinetry conceals storage and a hiding place below the countertop for a front-loading washer and dryer. The tile counter is suitable for sorting and folding laundry.

"I have a beautiful, efficient laundry room steps from my bedroom," Valerie says. "But the best part is that no one suspects that's what it is. They think it is just a fabulous period bathroom."

WHIMSICAL PORCELAIN FAUCET HANDLES SERVE AS KNOBS ON THE LAUNDRY CABINET DOORS.

A SHOWER CURTAIN ADDS SOFT TEXTURE TO OFFSET THE HARD, SMOOTH TILE.

BIFOLD DOORS ON THE LOWER CABINETS REVEAL THE WASHER AND DRYER.

BEACH SCENE

A REFURBISHED MEDICINE CABINET HOLDS TOWELS
AND SOAPS. A STORAGE CABINET ABOVE DOES DOU-
BLE DUTY WITH DISPLAY SPACE ON ITS TOP SURFACE.
BOTANICAL PRINTS ACCENT THE CALMING COLORS.

ANTIQUE WALL SCONCES WITH THE ORIGINAL GLASS
CAST LIGHT ON THE MEDICINE CABINET AND SAL-
VAGED PEDESTAL SINK.

Equal portions ocean inspiration and 1940s cottage fashion mix in a Colorado master bathroom. While the
mountains are closer than the sea, the textures, colors,
and finishes in the two styles combine comfortably to create a breezy scene. "The two concepts are easy to marry,"
interior designer Michelle Riviera says.

Space was carved out of an ill-conceived 1980s addition
for the new two-room bath; Riviera also appropriated
room from a carpeted second-floor landing. One room
holds the bathtub, stand-alone shower, and a terry cloth-

covered bench. The other contains a sink and toilet. Soft accents fill both spaces and no door separates the unusual arrangement. That "allowed for fun things to happen," Riviera says.

Riviera treated each element in the bathroom as a piece of furniture and let the homeowner's fondness for warm-weather colors and fabrics guide architectural details and the soothing palette. Custom-made white wainscoting from board-and-batten panels anchors the lower half of the walls, accented with a wash of sea blues and greens on the upper wall sections and storage pieces. Fine white cotton sheers shield the generous double-hung windows. Along with the shade of a large elm outside, the sheers allow sunlight and airy breezes to filter into the room, but maintain privacy.

Vintage pieces, scoured from salvage yards and antiques shops found new life in the bathroom; that investment in the small details sets the nostalgic 1940s impression. A medical-supply cabinet, repaired and repainted, stores toiletries. Sconces cast light on an above-sink cabinet. The vaguely Art Deco platform base of the antique, porcelain-lined, cast-iron tub sits neatly on the floor's tiny hexagonal tiles. Old-fashioned nickel-plated tub and sink fixtures were some of the few brand-new additions.

Bathroom necessities sit perfectly on the wide surface of the pedestal sink, another salvage find. Above the tub a vintage chandelier hangs from the high ceiling and "feels grand," Riviera says. A bench next to the tub, accented with a vintage linen throw pillow, offers a perch for after the bath. Framed antique botanicals and a circular window, reminiscent of the beachfront, finish off the sea scene.

The mix—call it 1940s beach decor—is a sanctuary that works.

"I think baths should be retreats," Riviera says. "They should be places you can go to restore yourself."

WHITE COTTON SHEERS, COMBINED WITH THE SHADE OF AN ELM TREE, PROVIDE THE ONLY NEEDED SECLUSION. THE TUB'S PLATFORM BASE MESHES PERFECTLY WITH THE REST OF THE ROOM'S VINTAGE FINDS.

NEW NICKEL-PLATED SINK FIXTURES MATCH THE ROOM'S STYLE. THE SURFACE OF THE PEDESTAL SINK AFFORDS GENEROUS SPACE FOR SOAP AND OTHER TOILETRIES.

THE DESIGN OF THE HANDHELD SHOWER WAND ACCENTS THE COTTAGE LOOK.

Inspired by old French furniture, the vanity features a pitted travertine counter and a shelf running the length of the mirror.

Fitted with frameless glass doors and unpolished marble, the unobtrusive shower is convenient without distracting from the tub and vanity.

Originally designed to be a comforting parental retreat from the trials of family life, this master bath proved to be successful beyond the homeowners' intentions. The room is so inviting that it has become a gathering place for the whole family.

With its vintage ambience and gracious seating space the sunlit room welcomes not only the homeowners but their children as well. "We pictured a place where we could hide out," owner Judy Zafran says. "That's why it's so comfy."

Abundant natural light and earthen textures make this bath a serene destination point rather than a simple utility. "I wanted windows top to bottom," Zafran says. Three French doors dominate an entire wall, making the space seem larger and allowing a privileged view of a rose garden. To highlight the garden view, the room features a subdued, warm palette using neutral stone flooring, ivory Roman shades, and golden hues. "We wanted to soften [the room] with casual elegance and colors that were harmonious with the outside," designer Mark Cutler says.

Thanks to Cutler, the custom-made vanity lends rustic elegance. Modeled on antique French cupboards, the cabinets are painted with a stripped, crackle-glaze finish that provides an aged look. A pitted travertine counter tops the vanity. A shelf just below the mirror gives the vanity the detail of real furniture. "The little shelf over the countertop is something you often see on old French washstands," Cutler says.

While the bath has a spacious, glass-enclosed shower, a classic white, claw-foot tub serves as the room's centerpiece and the focal point for a seating area. A toilet alcove occupies an old doorway and clears space for more furniture. A convenient table stand beside the tub and a reupholstered chair occupy a sunlit corner, transforming the bath into a place of rest and reflection. A slipcover stitched together from soft terry cloth towels makes the chair—a curbside cast-off—even more inviting. Epitomizing the room's casual staying power, the slipcover may easily be laundered and returned to the chair.

The cozy confluence of tables, fabric, and sunlight makes this room as much a sitting room as a bath. Speakers in the ceiling provide music or news as the family prepares for the day or merely enjoys the afternoon sunlight. "I do whatever I can in here," Zafran says. "At every time of the day you get wonderful light. It works perfectly for us."

BORDERING THE HONED MARBLE FLOOR AND IMITATING THE LOOK OF AN AREA RUG, A MOSAIC OF BROKEN LIMESTONE CREATES A RUSTIC TEXTURE.

NESTLED BY ONE OF THE FRENCH DOORS AND DRAPED IN A SLIPCOVER MADE OF TERRY CLOTH TOWELS, THIS SECOND-HAND CHAIR OFFERS AN ATTRACTIVE SPOT FOR REFLECTION.

7 AGED BY DESIGN

Whether you live in a period home with a bath in need of an update or are just a fan of the style, re-creating a retro look is definitely in vogue. Arts and Crafts and Art Deco remain two of the most popular design styles. If you long for simplicity, a Craftsman-inspired bath may be your ideal. Incorporate natural elements, such as broad, horizontal bands of wood in warm tones. Add tile and painted walls in a natural, earthy palette. If you prefer the understated, clean glamour of metal and clear bold lines, look to Art Deco-inspired spaces. Shiny metal, plastic, and clear glass are materials of choice, and brilliant blues, greens, and other dramatic hues are sure to perk up your morning.

Craftsman Revival

Take Craftsman-era details and update them with modern amenities, and the result is the luxury of this master bathroom retreat.

Turn-of-the-20th-century character starts with the dual marble vanities. Supported by stylish mahogany legs, their scale and form echo old-time laundry sinks. Storage comes from an adjacent built-in mahogany cupboard accented with vintage hardware.

Mahogany ties together past and present, in baseboards and the wide bands that wrap around mirrors and extend to the windows. A grid pattern—a common Craftsman detail—appears in mahogany on the tub surround and lighted overhead soffit. The rich wood tones warmly counterpoint the soft neutral of the marble floor and white walls.

While the lines are simple, the comforts are pure elegance. A corner whirlpool tub offers room to sit back and enjoy the mountain views, while a roomy walk-in shower envelops bathers in spray or steam. Motorized window blinds, opened with either a wall switch or remote control, adjust light and privacy, and a wall-mounted TV provides yet another luxurious amenity.

It's a bathroom that works well, for both function and beauty.

"People like the fact that Craftsman is a simple style," says the bath's interior designer, Judy Robins. "It is a very easygoing style to live with."

DUAL VANITIES, REMINISCENT OF OLD-STYLE LAUNDRY SINKS, PROVIDE AMPLE SURFACE SPACE FOR BATHING NECESSITIES. AN ADJACENT MAHOGANY STORAGE CABINET ECHOES THE VINTAGE FEEL.

ELEGANT APPOINTMENTS—FROM A MARBLE FLOOR TO MAHOGANY ACCENTS—INVITE LUXURIOUS BATHING. A CORNER WHIRLPOOL TUB IS LIT FROM ABOVE WITH FIXTURES IN AN OVERHEAD SOFFIT.

BUILT-IN FURNITURELIKE STORAGE
MAHOGANY ACCENTS THROUGHOUT
BLINDS OPERATED BY SWITCH AND REMOTE
MARBLE FLOOR AND COUNTERTOPS

Home-Crafted

In an older home finding a balance between new, convenient space and maintaining stylistic authenticity is often a series of disappointing compromises. Chris and Hennie Jones' 1912 Arts and Crafts bungalow offered added concern. The Vancouver home, a splendid example of the style, is cited by the Vancouver Heritage Advisory Committee for its English Arts and Crafts elements.

"We wanted to make changes," Chris says, "but only if they were done in the same architectural style."

With two teenage daughters, but only one bathroom on the main floor, alterations seemed to be a necessity, but adding to a "heritage" structure was complicated. The home's classic hipped roof, shed dormers, and casement windows meant alterations could not be made to the front without disrupting the historical integrity. The homeowners, however, were willing to not only maintain the look of their architectural treasure, but to enhance it.

Architect Allan Diamond appreciated this level of dedication. After he created the new space by expanding dormers out the back and side, the homeowners set about finding the crucial, period-appropriate details.

"They did lots of homework," Diamond says of the homeowners. "There aren't many clients who are willing to drive to Seattle or Portland to find the person to hand-make tiles."

Persistence, however, pays off. Designed to resemble the original tile work in other period homes, the shower features artisan-crafted tiles on the floor, border, and delicate frieze. The windows and door are the work of a European master craftsman. The windows on the main floor served as the pattern base for the replicas, ornate leaded-glass windows. A pocket door saves space, and the door frames echo the leaded-glass design, allowing

RATHER THAN A VANITY THE OWNERS SELECTED AN ANTIQUE PERIOD CABINET WITH REVEAL SHELVES AND A PULL-OUT TRAY.

HANDCRAFTED TILE IN THE SHOWER EVOKES THE ORIGINAL ARTS AND CRAFTS DETAILS.

FOUND IN A SPECIALTY SHOP, A PEDESTAL SINK WITH BRASS FAUCETS MAINTAINS A VINTAGE SENSIBILITY.

natural light to move through the bath.

The quest for vintage authenticity often required patience and a high level of antique shopping expertise. The light fixtures, window casements, and latches were culled from shops throughout the Pacific Northwest. Brass pieces—featured in a rebuilt period toilet, the tub's English-style hand sprayer, and a sink pedestal that was found in a Toronto specialty shop—allow old and new to coordinate. Replacing a traditional vanity, an Arts-and-Crafts wooden cabinet provides a distinct sense of stylistic completeness.

The Arts and Crafts movement, as exhibited in this bungalow, sought high quality through unpretentious, organic-inspired design and natural materials. Wood, natural light, and simple details created a splendid balance. For those early architects—as for these homeowners—it was rewarding and inspiring.

THE NEW TUB FAUCET IS DESIGNED TO RESEMBLE OLD BRITISH-STYLE HANDHELD SPRAYERS.

A NEW VINTAGE-INSPIRED CLAW-FOOT TUB COMPLEMENTS THE STRONG PERIOD ELEMENTS IN THE SHOWER AND WINDOWS.

NATURAL LIGHT IS ABLE TO STREAM THROUGH ORNATE LEADED-GLASS WINDOWS AND THE POCKET DOOR THAT LEADS TO THE ADJACENT ROOM.

WOOD AND WARMTH

By enclosing a former deck, Lynne and Steve Pearson created a spacious third-floor guest bath that dishes out hearty elegance. Designer Lou Ann Bauer focused on their home's Arts and Crafts style to infuse the space with warmth and personality.

The floor's 12×12-inch slate tiles are punctuated with copper insets and heated with radiant elements to establish a warm feel and an earthy look. The glass shower enclosure expands the bath visually and keeps the slate that lines the shower walls and floor viewable. "The slate has very beautiful colors in it," Steve says.

Windows and woodwork play prominent roles. Cherry cabinets designed with simple recessed panels and black hardware echo the look of the Mission-style furniture common to the Craftsman era. An adjoining window seat offers a comfortable cushion as well as drawers that pull out from beneath the seat for additional storage. Two tall windows flank a transom above the sink.

"Because it's on the third floor," Bauer explains, "it's like a treehouse bathroom—very natural and very peaceful."

LARGE 12×12-INCH SLATE TILES CLIMB THE SHOWER WALLS AT A DIAGONAL FOR INTEREST. THE GLASS ENCLOSURE ALLOWS VIEWS OF THE TILES FROM ELSEWHERE IN THE BATH. FROM INSIDE THE SHOWER THE VISTA INCLUDES THE TREETOPS OUTSIDE THE THIRD-FLOOR WINDOWS.

CABINETS TUCKED UNDER THE COZY CUSHIONED WINDOW SEAT OFFER STORAGE SPACE FOR TOWELS.

WIDE WOODWORK AND THE VANITY'S CHERRY CABINETRY WITH SIMPLE RECESSED PANEL DOORS AND DRAWERS FIT THE CRAFTSMAN STYLE THE HOMEOWNERS WANTED TO MAINTAIN.

PRAIRIE RETREAT

Like a magician pulling tricks from a tall top hat, residential designer Geno Benvenuti put the tools of his trade to work in his home's spalike master bathroom. The end result is a personal sanctuary.

"There are three areas critical to today's lifestyles: a family room to relax, a bedroom to relax, and a bathroom to relax," Geno says.

The retreat replaced a spare bedroom in the 1908 Prairie-style home. Its design revolves around two beautiful hardworking elements: finely crafted furniturelike built-ins and exquisitely composed tilework. White oak, with a tight vertical grain of quarter- and rift-cuts, forms cabinets around dual sinks. A curved wood apron fronting each sink softens the otherwise static edges. Slim cupboardlike medicine cabinets flank recessed mirrors, hiding toiletries and providing storage. Crown molding tops cupboards, shelves, and the mirror area, tying together the vanity space.

White oak continues on the face of the whirlpool tub surround, while dark-color granite on vanity surfaces and a backsplash against the tub anchors those lighter tones. Open shelving just behind the head of the bathtub holds decorative items and towels.

Throughout the room, tilework in deep blues and lighter greens complements the oak, starting with a simple subwaylike tile on the vanity wall. In the rest of the bathroom Geno chose tiles from two companies, mixed them together, and fashioned fanciful patterns to create a range of visual interest. Scroll patterns around the mirrors represent a water theme, and the tile decoration continues in the shower.

Above a bench in the oversize space, a mural accented with a bit of yellow creates a focal point to enjoy while bathers bask in a flood of steam. Radiant heat below the cream-color floor tiles warms the floor and the feet. Scattered animal-shape tiles add a bit of whimsy. Natural light bathes the space through a window behind the tub.

OPEN SHELVING, ALSO IN WHITE OAK, HOLDS NECESSITIES TO COMPLETE THE SPA EXPERIENCE; THE WINDOW WAS PART OF THE OLD SPARE BEDROOM. A SCROLL PATTERN AROUND THE RECESSED MIRRORS CONTINUES THE WATER THEME.

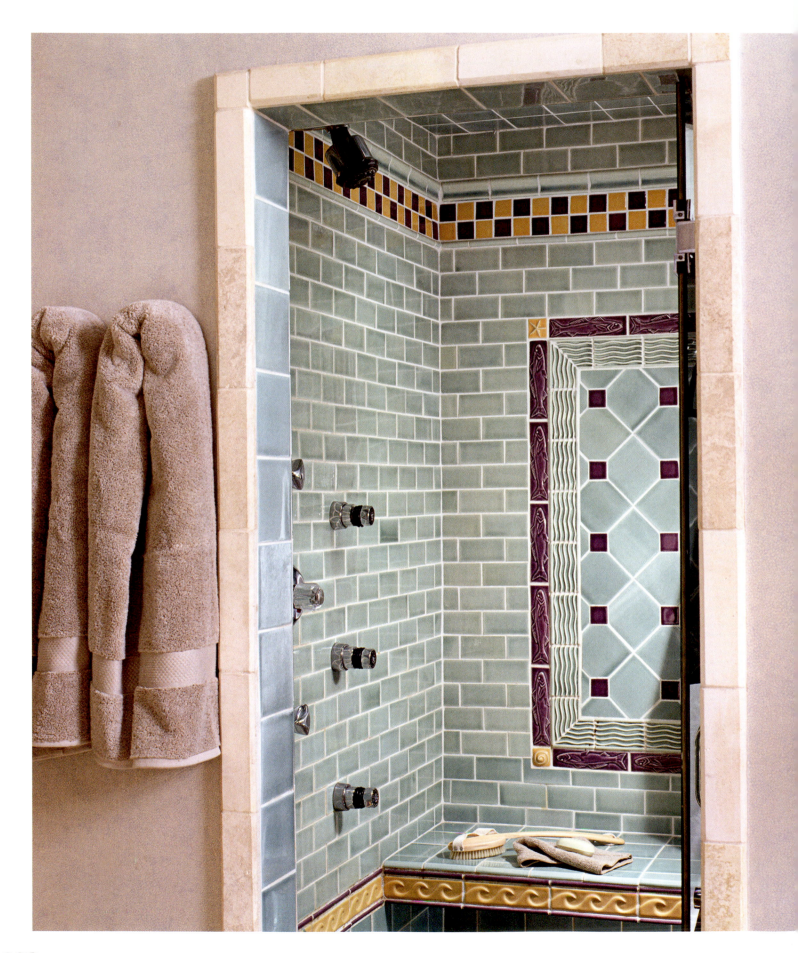

Each bath element is more than just utilitarian; all functions contribute equally to the spa experience. While the family lost a bedroom, it was a trade-off well worth making, for the space is more than just a room to shower and shave.

"It sets the mood for how you start the day and for how you end the night," Geno says.

A TILE MURAL IN SEA-INSPIRED COLORS SITS ABOVE A SHOWER BENCH. KNOBS IN THE OVERSIZE SPACE CONTROL STEAM.

SLIM COUNTER CABINETS HIDE TOILETRIES. A CURVED APRON FRONT BREAKS UP THE HORIZONTAL LINES OF THE FURNITURELIKE BUILT-INS.

HANDMADE TILE INSERTS—LIKE THIS FROG—BREAK UP THE EXPANSE OF CREAM-COLOR FLOOR TILE.

When interior designer Leslie Harris stripped the bath in her 1928 Los Angeles home down to the studs, all that was left was a window. That single detail was just what she needed to mesh a spirited, timeless design with a flash of updated personality.

Leslie saluted tradition in the 5×10-foot bath, part of a former servants' quarters, with furniturelike pieces. Warm, solid cherry forms the open vanity, mirror, and built-in storage shelves. While vaguely old school, the metallic nickel finishes on sink, faucets, and fittings add definite 21st-century sparkle, as do the contemporary wall sconces. Open shelves below the sink and in the adjacent wall niche hold bathing necessities without adding the clutter of doors and drawers. Metallic bands on the mirror tie the pieces together.

Golden crackle-finish field tiles pave the three walls surrounding the tub, as well as the surround. All eyes turn toward the backlit niche above the tub; its white tile frame, which mimics the look of framed artwork, bounces light from the adjacent window into the rest of the room.

What was an undistinguished space now spans old and new, adding warmth, color, and drama to Leslie's home. It's a design that definitely welcomed the bathroom into the new century.

THE SPARKLING FINISH ON THE FIXTURES ALLUDES TO THE ELEGANCE AND EXCESS OF THE CENTURY OF THE HOME'S BIRTH. SHELVES RECESSED INTO THE WALL KEEP BATH NECESSITIES CLOSE AT HAND.

TILE PAVES THE TUB SURROUND AND WALLS, BUT ALL EYES MOVE TOWARD THE FRAMED BACKLIT NICHE. REFLECTING OFF THE WHITE TILES, LIGHT BOUNCES EVEN FURTHER INTO THE ROOM.

PLEASANT PAIR

Connie and Gary Kelley's bath is an ideal example that achieving a retro look doesn't have to mean rigidly adhering to specific period designs. The bath pleasingly combines Arts and Crafts sensibilities and Art Deco flair, mixed with the couple's penchant for arty elements.

The old bathroom located off the main hallway in the 1939 bungalow wasn't roomy enough for the busy parents to get ready at the same time, nor was it attractive to guests. Fixtures lined up against the walls—shower stall, toilet, and tub on one side, sink and storage chest on the other—created a bowling alley effect in the middle. In a 9½×6-foot room there was little space left.

After four years of squeezing through the unattractive space, Gary spotted a Philippe Starck pear-wood vanity pictured in a magazine. The clean-lined cabinet with the sink bowl on top of the counter provided the impetus for change.

Designer Tina Barclay was charged with creating an attractive, functional bath around the vanity within the existing space. To increase function, Barclay gutted the room and reconfigured the plumbing. The bathtub and shower were positioned at the far end of the room, freeing floor space in the vanity area.

A border of 6-inch-square William Morris-style custom tiles tops the glass-tile walls. "Most of [the Kelleys'] furniture is more Craftsman-inspired, so I needed a link [to the rest of the house]," Barclay says. The vibrant cobalt blue sconces, shimmering tiles, and simple geometric lines are all a nod to Art Deco style: a match with results that make everyone happy.

The off-center faucet reminds the homeowners of a tabletop fountain.

Details such as a magnifying mirror and reflective 1-inch-square glass tiles in sea green help achieve a spalike quality.

A frameless stationary glass wall extends more than halfway across the shower stall, enclosing the shower without blocking light and views.

On the shower floor, cobalt blue glass tiles with a multicolor border were custom-colored to match the William Morris-style tiles at the ceiling.

Whimsical details such as the frog tile personalize the bath.

WET AREA DEFINED BY FRAMELESS GLASS WALL

OFF-CENTER SINK FAUCET

MAGNIFYING MIRROR IN VANITY AREA

8 SUIT YOUR STYLE

Perhaps one of the most influential design trends today is creating a space uniquely yours—a particularly noteworthy influence in a room as personal as the bath. Take your inspiration from a favorite object or destination. In this chapter you'll find a bath inspired by an Egyptian iron chandelier that evoked fond childhood memories of Cairo markets for the homeowner. Re-create a slice of your favorite getaway to soothe away daily cares when you're homebound. Or delight in an eclectic mix of materials and styles woven together by your favorite treasures. As well as the baths here, look to the other rooms in your home, and to clothing, art, and collectibles for inspiration.

LOOK HOMEWARD

Despite its immediate utilitarian purpose, a bathroom doesn't need to sacrifice personality and livability for function. With combined spaces and decorative details a bath may be so inviting that it becomes a place as much for reflection and conversation as personal grooming.

Applying this philosophy, designer Mary Emmerling gives this urban loft a dose of nostalgic, homeward-looking charm. Through an infusion of character-rich details and decor the space suggests a front parlor more than a bathroom. A restrained use of fixtures and built-in structures allows a relaxed space for decorative accessories. Rather than relying on slick surfaces, this bath features well-worn objects, fabrics, and ornamental displays to personalize the atmosphere.

While the bath possesses all the expected necessities, fixtures incorporate into unexpected and comforting elements. The sink is charmingly installed in the top of a chest of drawers. This furniture and plumbing fusion is not only novel but creates a feeling of domestic comfort. A recessed niche leaves the shower and claw-foot tub combination open to the rest of the room, but maintains a degree of formal separation. Reminiscent of a tea table the vanity features a graceful linen runner and a cake platter that holds grooming accessories.

An abundant use of textiles—including rugs, curtains, and table covers—provides a comforting, tactile dimension. With a dark blue satin stripe design, the walls present a lush, refined richness. Decorative items such as perfume bottles, aged family photos, collectibles, and antique linens produce a sense of meaningful accumulation and personalize the room. Emmerling utilizes handbags, antique-appearing lamps, straw baskets, and old snapshots to evoke lived-in, nostalgic charm. Monograms on the vanity runner and the cafe-style shower

FRAMING THE CLASSIC CLAW-FOOT TUB, A RECESSED NICHE PROVIDES A COZY ENCLOSURE WHILE LEAVING THE TUB OPEN TO THE ROOM.

curtain add a warm and distinctly personal element.

Dark blue hues set an elegant tone, but a mix of styles and elements soften the overall effect, making this space interesting and inviting. This purposeful clutter also creates a playful, intriguing atmosphere. As Gary McKay, a member of Emmerling's design team says, the stylistic combination should "look as if you got it from 10 different flea markets over a period of years."

Thanks to two windows positioned behind the sink/dresser and the tub, the blue mood is lightened even further by broad swaths of natural light. All these recognizable, well-loved details make a bath more than a charming showpiece. The room becomes a pleasing, personal collage that suggests one can, indeed, go home again.

WITH AGED SNAPSHOTS, ANTIQUE UTENSILS, A QUILTED SLIPCOVER, AND A LINEN RUNNER, THE VANITY EVOKES COMFORTABLE, NOSTALGIC ELEGANCE.

REJECTING TYPICAL BATH FIXTURES, THE SINK IS INSTALLED INTO THE TOP OF A DRESSER, HIGHLIGHTING THE ROOM'S CHARMING MIX OF ELEMENTS.

RANCH REDUX

No one would guess that the past life of Ken and Jacki Widder's 1960s Southern California ranch contained gloomy, claustrophobic spaces, dreary woodwork, and outdated colors. But that was the case when the couple bought the home, enamored of its ocean and valley views, cathedral ceilings, and windows, doors, and skylights.

Together with a friend, interior designer Cynthia Lambert, the couple embarked step-by-step on a whole-house remodeling. Along the way they dramatically transformed the navy blue tile-clad master bathroom into a sunny, spacious haven.

Not much of the room's old life remains; the space was gutted, and new fixtures, fittings, and traditional-style cabinetry were installed. Two rooms make up the suite—a bathing/showering area and grooming space.

In the bathing area repeating patterns, tiles, and colors provide the design foundation. Four-inch-square tumbled-marble tiles pave the walls, matched by 12-inch squares that cover the floor and deck of the deep, ground-level, oval whirlpool tub. Tile also paves the adjacent open sunken shower.

A cream-color abstract mural made from patterned ceramic tiles extends across the bath and shower area, breaking up the strong geometry of the squares. Its swirls and whirls mimic the tub's massaging bubbles; a matching tile border sits low against the wall. Whitewash lightens the rafters and ceiling beams, and skylights flood the space with dappled light from morning until night. Neutral tones—soft beige in the tile, soft brown on the rafters, and white in the mural and tub—reflect even more light into the corners.

Just steps from the bathing area, a separate grooming space is cheerful and serene. Awash in pale-yellow paint, it's a welcome transition to the rich textures and muted tones of the bath space. A pair of antique 19th-century pine doors inspired the design of a 13-foot-long vanity, with dual grooming areas and center sit-down cosmetic counter. The doors front the tall pine storage cupboard, which holds linens and laundry hampers, at the vanity's end. Undercounter wood built-ins provide further ample storage, and a large mirror reflects light from the pendent fixtures, wall sconces, and clerestory windows. Another short walkway links the two rooms with the master bedroom.

The couple took a well-planned approach in their whole-house remodeling. Their vision gave them not only the bathroom, but the house of their dreams.

TILE LINES THE BENCH AND WALLS OF THE SUNKEN SHOWER. DAPPLED LIGHT CASTS A SHADOW AGAINST WHITEWASHED RAFTERS.

SUBSTANTIAL FIXTURES FLOOD THE GENEROUS WHIRLPOOL TUB. A WALL MURAL BREAKS UP THE SOFT NEUTRALS OF THE MARBLE TILE. LARGER SQUARES OF THE SAME MARBLE PAVE THE TUB'S DECK.

GENEROUS SURFACES ON THE 13-FOOT-LONG VANITY PROVIDE PLENTY OF ROOM FOR GROOMING AND COSMETIC NEEDS. THE DOUBLE DOORS ON THE CUPBOARD—ANTIQUE STORE FINDS—WERE THE INSPIRATION FOR THE CONSTRUCTION OF THE BUILT-INS.

A SHORT WALKWAY OFF THE GROOMING AREA CONNECTS THE MASTER BEDROOM. AN ORIGINAL BUILT-IN DRESSER STORES EVERYDAY CLOTHES.

Natural Selections

With Seattle's famous emerald scenery and infamous lack of sunshine, designer and builder Kirk Derby wanted to capture as much outdoor beauty and natural light as possible in a new master bath. Seeking to create an earthy retreat that incorporates the scenery around them, Derby and his wife, Karna Sundby, wanted to merge their new bath with the elements of the Pacific Northwest.

"We can see the Olympic Mountains here, and we have a really beautiful English garden in the back," Kirk says. "I wanted to bring that right into that bathroom wherever I could."

A repositioned roof with new dormers enlarged the space and provided the opportunity to install a skylight.

Partnered with new windows on two sides of the shower and above the tub, natural light illuminates the room even on subdued, overcast days. A glass door leads to a new balcony, permitting the homeowners to enjoy fresh air and a panoramic view.

Tumbled marble creates a soothing, earthen texture on the walls, floor, and bathing enclosures. This tile possesses the elegance of smoother stone, but provides visual warmth and a worn, less slippery texture. Building on this use of intriguing stone patterns, tropical rain-forest marble forms the countertops. With its rich, wood tones, the vanity complements the natural theme and is designed to resemble freestanding furniture. Adding his own handcrafted touch, Derby designed,

Used to create a serene space for bathing, tumbled marble presents a worn, comfortable texture with a visually interesting appearance.

A balcony off the bath completes the room's coordination with the outdoor environment.

A glass door, window, and skylight allow sunshine to illuminate the vanity's blend of wood and stone.

fired, and glazed the sinks himself.

With the visual foundation of the comforting, organic stone textures, the fixture arrangement maximizes openness. The generous whirlpool tub pairs with an open, dual-head shower that features a low enclosure wall. To maintain a clear, uncluttered fluidity, two 8-foot walls surround the toilet, creating a water closet that is efficiently tucked out of sight.

The room opens up to the out-of-doors and draws in every ray of sunshine, while offering small conveniences for a cool climate. Radiant heat warms the floor tiles, helping keep the bathroom a very pleasant temperature. "Putting underfloor heating in this bathroom was the smartest decision I have ever made," Derby says.

Behind the vanity the couple made space for a small sauna, ensuring that this master bath would be a comforting retreat, no matter what weather graces their balcony, rain or shine.

LOW WALLS AND TWO WINDOWS AROUND THE SHOWER MAINTAIN AN OPENNESS AND CONNECTION TO THE SURROUNDINGS.

EARTHY HUES AND VISUALLY INTERESTING MARBLE ON THE VANITY HIGHLIGHT THE NATURAL TONE OF THE ROOM.

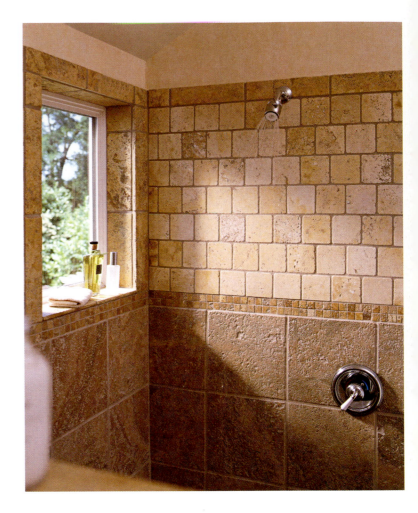

TRANQUIL WATERS

To drain away the stress caused by hectic days that include keeping up with her 6- and 7-year-old daughters, Julie Malek made a commitment to treat herself to a nightly bubble bath. "At night when I get in the bath, I feel like I'm escaping," she says. "It's the perfect getaway right here at home."

So when Julie and her husband, Rick Kornfeld, added a master suite to their 1920s Dutch Revival home, a comfy bath was the first item on the list. The couple also wanted the entire bath to evoke a calm, meditative feeling, so they enlisted the help of interior designer Kristi Dinner to build a retreat with style.

"The way you create harmony is by including elements that complement each other. Everything works together to achieve a balance," Dinner says. "That's what makes this space so striking."

A number of opposing forces combine to create balance in the bath. Cool, watery greens pair with dark wood tones. Smooth tiles on the vanity and floor play against textured beaded-board cabinets and bamboo-covered windows. Asian-style design melds with a French-inspired vanity and wall tiles that recall those found in Paris Metro stations.

To evoke serenity, plenty of light and a lack of color were additional requirements. A skylight and double windows brighten the north-facing room, and a large mirror, which doubles as a medicine cabinet, reflects sunlight off the walls. To contain any mess, a built-in cabinet stores linens in an otherwise unused and narrow space, and the custom-made vanity, inspired by a furniture piece Dinner saw in France, holds everything from washcloths to Rick's watch collection. Cubbies by the tub ensure that shampoos, bath salts, and candles are within reach.

While the room looks as if it came together effortlessly, deciding on all the details took plenty of weekly meet-

SATIN-FINISH NICKEL FAUCETS BOAST A SLEEK DESIGN THAT COMBINES FORM AND FUNCTION.

A SPECIAL STORAGE STATION DESIGNED ESPECIALLY FOR TIMEPIECES HOUSES RICK'S PRIZED WATCH COLLECTION.

THE HOMEOWNERS DROPPED THEIR REQUIREMENT FOR DUAL SINKS, OPTING INSTEAD FOR ONE LARGE SINK THAT RESEMBLES A BASIN SITTING ATOP THE CABINET.

- Contrasting design elements for impact
- Lined compartment drawers
- Custom-made storage pieces

ings. Even choosing the perfect tub became a project. "There's nothing worse than building a bathroom and having a bath that's not comfortable," Dinner says. "So I had the homeowners meet me several times and get in the tubs we were looking at—actually take off their shoes and get in. We spent several lunch hours doing that!"

Julie found the right tub, and now it's a pivotal part of her nightly retreat.

BESIDES BALANCING COLORS AND TEXTURES IN THE MASTER BATH, INTERIOR DESIGNER KRISTI DINNER ALSO BALANCED THE BUDGET BY CHOOSING COST-EFFICIENT MATERIALS, SUCH AS THE LIMESTONE FLOOR AND TILE FOR THE SHOWER AND TUB DECK.

A STORAGE CABINET TUCKED INTO THE NARROW SPACE NEAR THE TUB CONTAINS TOWELS, SHEETS, AND OTHER LINENS.

Behind the Curtain

When Chicago architects Claudia Skylar and James Mastro moved out of their Victorian-era home to try their hand at transforming a two-story commercial building, they took particular care in tackling their private quarters. The goal, Claudia says, was to create a master suite that was "loftlike and modern, yet cozy and seductive."

"We agonized over this project to come up with something that fit the way we really live," Claudia says. "We finally came to the conclusion that a bath didn't have to look like a locker room or a warehouse to work well, and that there were a lot of things we could leave out—including doors."

To do this Claudia and James cleared their minds of conventional design notions. "We tried to look at the space as if we were Martians and not in the least influenced by current style or conventional thinking," Claudia says. "What we wanted was a bath that was fully integrated into the master bedroom without actually being in the master bedroom."

Working with a century-old building in Chicago that had once been a repair shop for horse-drawn carriages freed the couple from having to work around traditional interior spaces. "Integration" meant minimizing the boundary between the bedroom and bath with a single partition flanked by two openings. More importantly, they succeed in civilizing the look of requisite bathroom fixtures by strategically using what Claudia calls "non-bathroomy" materials—and on occasion making them

In addition to a window of its own, the bath benefits from a wide, door-free opening on each side of the sink wall. This allows light to stream in from the adjacent master bedroom.

Fixed mirror panels recessed 2 inches into the curry-color wall give the appearance of windows. Half-inch squares of mosaic tiles were used for to-the-floor backsplashes.

disappear altogether behind folds of bronze silk.

James employed his own considerable woodworking skills to fashion the mahogany enclosure for the tub. The warm color and fine grain of the mahogany take a chill off the white porcelain and give a furniturelike quality to the requisite bathroom fixture. In addition the mahogany elegantly balances the taupe-painted brick wall, which recalls the building's industrial roots. The reproduction French-style chest and antique gold-leaf mirror located in the toilet alcove are other elements of finery rarely found in bathrooms.

To maintain the notion of a bath as an elegant, visually appealing space in its own right, the couple also made notable omissions. For starters, they rejected a glass shower door. Instead a nylon liner hangs from its own track between the shower walls, providing a clear view of the "limestone-tiled shower that reads like a beautiful wall," Claudia says.

The curtain doesn't hide the sinks on the opposite wall. Yet even this area possesses a touch of style. Claudia and James decided against a double vanity, medicine cabinets, and an in-the-bath linen closet. "Originally, we planned a long vanity," Claudia says, "but the pedestal sinks are less intrusive. They don't fill up the space the way a built-in vanity does." Instead of mirrored medicine cabinets the couple chose recessed mirrors. "We realized we really didn't need a lot of in-the-bath storage,"

ATTRACTIVE CURVED FRONT CORNERS AND FLAT SURFACES FOR TOILETRIES DISTINGUISH THE PEDESTAL SINKS.

STAINLESS-STEEL CARTS KEEP ESSENTIAL GROOMING SUPPLIES CLOSE AT HAND AND CAN BE ROLLED TO THE SHOWER WHEN NEEDED.

CONTEMPORARY SINGLE-LEVER FAUCETS ARE EASY TO USE AND ECHO THE SHAPE OF THE STAINLESS-STEEL STORAGE CARTS.

PEDESTAL SINKS POSITIONED SIDE BY SIDE LEAVE AMPLE SPACE FOR TWO PEOPLE TO MANEUVER IN THE NARROW ROOM.

Claudia says. "There's a dressing table in the bedroom and a large linen/storage closet outside the bedroom." Two stainless-steel carts parked alongside the sinks keep essential grooming instruments close at hand.

As striking as the bathroom compartments are, however, the allure of the bath lies in how most of the area is

THE DARK, RICH WOOD OF THE MAHOGANY TUB ENCLOSURE PLAYS DOWN THE UTILITARIAN TUB AND ADDS AN ELEMENT OF HANDCRAFTSMANSHIP.

FOLDS OF BRONZE SILK COMPLETELY HIDE THE TUB, TOILET, AND SHOWER WHEN THE CURTAIN IS DRAWN.

instantly hidden with a sweep of the two silk curtain panels. This equally stunning oasis accomplishes what Claudia calls the greatest design challenge: "To design a bathroom that didn't look too bathroomy, and sometimes, as is the case with the tub and shower, to 'hide' things in plain site by using beautiful materials."

LIMESTONE TILE COVERS THE SHOWER'S ORIGINAL BRICK WALL, WHERE A BOARDED-UP WINDOW WAS TURNED INTO A PRACTICAL NICHE.

With four kids dominating the rest of their home, David and Merle Barack wanted a new master bath that was theirs alone. The new bath would be a personal retreat away from the chaos of daily life. "We wanted to have open spaces without a lot of junk in them," Merle says. "With four kids your house can get really trashed, so we wanted our bath to be clean and neat, but also a warm place to hang out."

While the remodeling would carve out a space away from everyone else, it would also have to balance the needs of each spouse, who each wanted a personal grooming space and individual sink. David needed a

TALL, COLUMNLIKE MAPLE CABINETS DIVIDE THE VANITY SPACES WITH CRISP, MODERN ARCHITECTURAL DETAIL.

GLASS VESSEL BASINS PARTNER WITH SLENDER WALL-MOUNTED FAUCETS, CREATING A CLEAN AND CONTEMPORARY ELEGANCE.

shower, and Merle wanted a bathtub. Merle preferred a clean, contemporary look, while David leaned toward a more traditional approach. The result is an inspired marriage of personalities in a shared personal space.

Though the room needed to feel open, the couple also wanted to maintain a sense of intimacy and comfort. In the finished result, the high, soaring ceilings are constrained by grand, classical arches that lead the eye to the whirlpool bath. Cradled in a mosaic tile alcove the tub space is the room's focal point. Combining classical traits and contemporary details, wood cabinets with drawers resemble columns. These features add grand architectural sensibility without overwhelming the openness.

The room strategically blends warm Mediterranean colors into a soothing composition. Yellows in the limestone flooring and honey-tone maple in the crisp, modern cabinets mix in harmony. Countering the muted surfaces on the wood and stone, the mosaic glass tiles contribute to a variety of textures while maintaining a unified color scheme.

Since the room lacks an outdoor window, frosted glass over the tub offers a creative alternative. Fluorescent backlighting creates a subdued and fresh illumination, while a skylight allows natural light to combine with the room's golden hues.

The design offers plenty of amenities for two. Maintaining a fluid openness, vanities on opposing walls feature slender, wall-mounted faucets and elegant, glass vessel basins. Tucked behind the maple cabinets, the toilet enclosure hides opposite a spacious, glass-walled shower that features an overhead, rain-style spray.

Inspired by cooperation rather than compromise, this luminous, comforting bath offers what the couple needed as individuals and as partners. "It's our little private island," Merle says.

ARCHES ANCHORED BY COLUMNLIKE CABINETS SOFTEN THE HIGH CEILINGS AND DRAW THE EYE TO THE WHIRLPOOL BATH AT THE END OF THE ROOM.

TUCKED FROM VIEW BEHIND THE CABINETS, THE BROAD GLASS ENCLOSURE OF THE SPACIOUS SHOWER MAINTAINS THE ROOM'S OPENNESS.

Teamwork

By putting their collective talents and design minds together, interior designer Sherry Hayslip and her architect husband, Cole Smith, Sr., reconfigured a master bathroom into a fitting tribute to their 1926 Dutch colonial home. Filled with easy-to-rotate furniture pieces, the bath mixes traditional elements and clean lines in a bright, fresh space.

"We decided it was time to do for ourselves what we do for clients every day—create a space that was totally us and totally comfortable," Sherry says.

There were parts of the old bathroom that the couple loved—its mosaic tile floor and arched ceiling—but mostly the cramped, too-small space needed an infusion of function and efficiency.

After five years, the couple reconfigured the bath and a maze of small closets to enlarge the area. New elements—windows, a barrel-vaulted ceiling, and arched French doors to the bedroom—increase the spaciousness.

A SILK LAMPSHADE SPARKLES AGAINST THE MOSAIC TILE CEILING.

ONE OF THE DUAL SINKS SITS ON A DEEP BROWN ANTIQUE DUTCH KLAPBUFFET. BEHIND THE VANITIES A MIRRORED WALL REFLECTS SUN FROM WINDOWS AND HANGING LIGHT FIXTURES.

ANTIQUE DRESSER AS VANITY

WALL OF MIRRORS FOR SPACIOUSNESS

MOSAIC TILE ON THE CEILING

BARREL-VAULTED CEILING

The simple, neutral palette illuminates the space, but allows the strength of materials to shine. The mix "made the bathroom functional and beautiful, still appropriate for the house, but much more like us," Sherry says.

It started as a simple bath renovation, but the project spurred the couple to tackle other projects as a team. "It's certainly much more fun," Sherry says.

A GLASS SHOWER DOOR, FITTED WITH AN ORNATE SILVER HANDLE, BOUNCES LIGHT FROM CORNER TO CORNER.

INSET INTO A NICHE IN THE BATHROOM, A BOOKCASE MAXIMIZES DISPLAY AND FLEXIBILITY.

THE PRETTY HANDMADE MOSAIC TILE IS VISIBLE BEHIND THE OPEN SHELVES; AT THE BOTTOM ORNATE PULLS DRESS UP THE DOOR FRONTS.

A mix of freestanding furniture and built-in storage maximizes the room's utility. An antique Dutch *klapbuffet*—massive in size but elegant in lines—takes an unexpected turn as vanity for one of the sinks. A second, more traditional-looking basin, with open shelving below, supplies a home for the second sink. Behind the two vanities a mirrored wall reflects light from the windows and the painted silk shades of the hanging lamps. A mahogany bookcase, tucked into a niche between a doorway and storage, adds room for an ever-changing display of photos and flowers. Adjacent to the shower, open upper shelves and double lower doors gather towels, soaps, and lotions.

Handcrafted finishes represent a distinct component of the room's appeal. On the floor, linen limestone squares create a diamond pattern; handmade art glass mosaic tiles sparkle on the ceiling, continuing down the wall behind the open storage. The mosaic runs into the shower, where limestone reappears on the floor and walls. Handmade iridescent glass in the French doors lets in light while maintaining privacy.

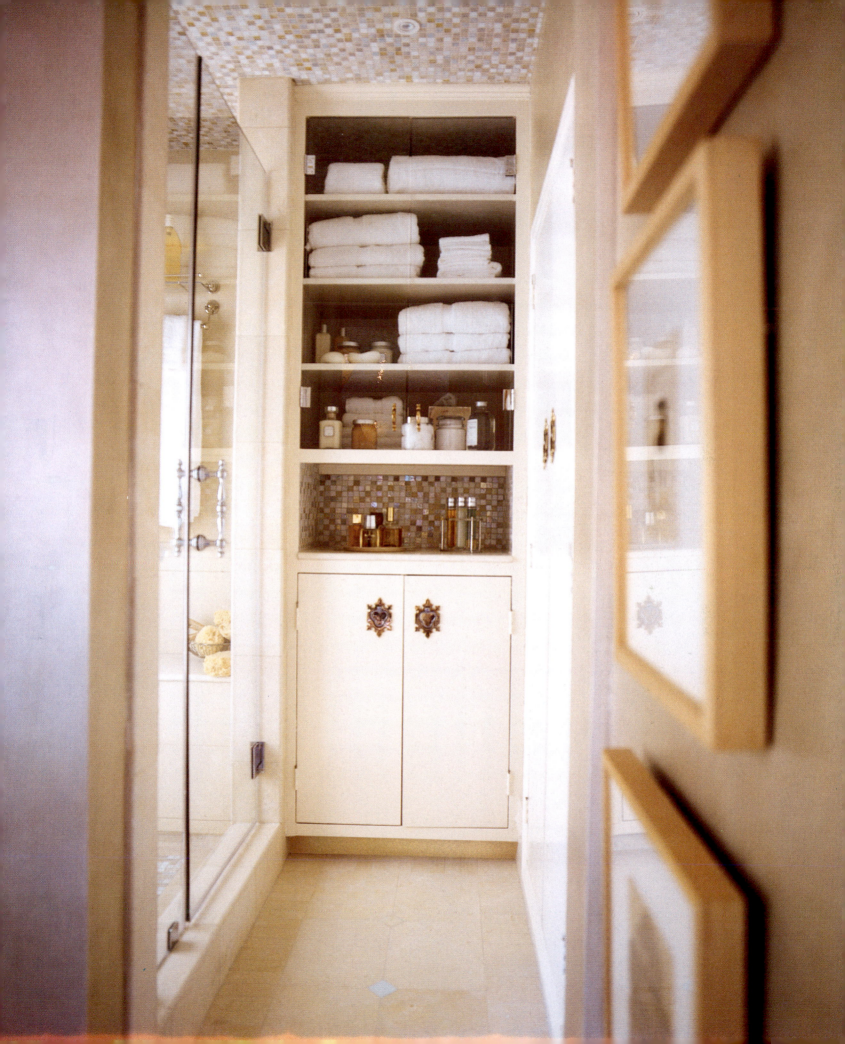

Egyptian Elegance

When Leigh O'Dell and Fotis Lycouridis decided to remodel the narrow, claustrophobic master bathroom in their 1937 fixer-upper, they wanted a larger room with more character and functionality. So they gleaned inspiration from Fotis' fond memories of the several years he lived in Egypt as a child. An iron Egyptian chandelier that once belonged to Fotis' parents became a focal point for their design plans, which involved re-creating facets of a favorite childhood home.

"That particular lamp always reminds me of Cairo and the big market that my parents got it from," Fotis says. "Putting something like that light in a place that you designed yourself . . . brings the family in. It makes the family be there."

Once they settled on a design, Leigh and Fotis replaced the existing vanity with an oak cabinet from a local antiques shop. The tiny, diamond-shape tiles that decorate the top of the vanity suggested the color scheme for the entire room. Neutral walls offer a subtle backdrop for tiles of Italian travertine in varying earth tones, which wrap the floor, lower portion of the walls, and tub enclosure. A tile-lined arch with the outline of a Middle Eastern minaret frames the tub and lends depth and openness. The motif continues in the arch over the toilet area and in the curved mirror over the sink.

When Leigh and Fotis couldn't find just the right tiles to make an accent band for the room, Fotis crafted his own. He cut the tiles into a starlike design, with a Moroccan look and the jewel-tone hues of an Oriental rug.

To suggest the eclectic mix of cultures found in a busy marketplace, Middle Eastern-theme accessories and art—such as a cup and soap holder from an Athens, Greece, flea market, and ceramic and metal Moroccan urns—decorate the space.

A POINTED ARCH ADDS DEPTH TO THE TUB ENCLOSURE. WALL HOOKS ON EITHER SIDE HOLD TOWELS AND ROBES.

THE TILE ARCH OVER THE TOILET ENCLOSURE EMULATES THE ARCH FRAMING THE TUB, LENDING DEPTH AND A SENSE OF PRIVACY.

A VINTAGE OAK CABINET, FOUND IN A LOCAL ANTIQUES SHOP, PROVIDES COLORFUL STORAGE IN THIS MIDDLE EASTERN-INSPIRED BATHROOM.

ECLECTIC MIX OF ACCESSORIES

MINARET MOTIF IN ARCHES AND MIRROR

ONE STANDOUT PIECE AS FOCAL POINT

The accent band of tile links the room's colors and architecturally influenced details, including the minaret-shape arches and the glass beads in the chandelier.

Small diamond-shape tiles decorate the top of the bathroom vanity and enhance the slate-color sink.

An Egyptian chandelier adds ambience to the bathroom. Outside, a 15-foot-tall laurel hedge provides a privacy screen, allowing the owners to skip window treatments and let light stream into the room.

Taking the Italian Renaissance as its inspiration, this bath embraces a forward-looking collaboration of independent thinking and artistic style. Designed to consider future changes in living circumstances, this room offers subtle but important reinterpretations of a bath's form and function.

Utilizing simple alternatives, the room features environmentally friendly and energy-efficient elements. Although it looks and feels like limestone, the floor tiles are a composite recycled from feldspar mining waste. Fluorescent lights, which are more energy-efficient compared with incandescent lamps, combine with sunshine. A broad, block-glass window offers both privacy and an abundance of natural illumination.

The bath is designed to provide elegant style and easy access for physically limited occupants. A low vanity with an extended sink basin and hidden plumbing allow an easy, unobstructed approach for wheelchairs. With only broken tile in the floor to designate a transition, the open shower has no barrier or threshold. Support bars and a handheld sprayer positioned low on the wall provide easy-to-reach convenience.

The final artistic touch is a collage of charcoal drawings reproducing the work of Leonardo daVinci. Like the master, this bath celebrates human endeavor, reimagining the everyday experience in a new way and embracing the art of independent thinking.

THE LOW, UNHINDERED SINK AND OPEN, BARRIER-LESS SHOWER MAKE THE BATH ARTFULLY CONVENIENT AND ACCESSIBLE.

THE MELDING OF SQUARE AND BROKEN TILE PROVIDES A VISUAL AND TACTILE TRANSITION FROM THE SINK AREA TO THE SHOWER.

POSITIONED NEAR daVINCI-INSPIRED ART, THE GRAB BAR IS BOTH SLEEKLY ELEGANT AND STOUTLY PRACTICAL FOR MOVING ABOUT THE SPACE.

OPEN SHOWER WITHOUT A BARRIER
LOW, UNOBSTRUCTED SINKS
RECYCLED TILE

Three murals frame the three sides of the tiled-in bath. Slightly angled sides and a side-mounted faucet with handheld sprayer on the tub allow for ease of use.

A frameless glass door allows light into the shower. The adjacent tub is shorter than standard, but still comfortable for a good soak.

Lars Jensen and Geoff Martin brought their professional talents home to roost for a masterful seascape in their 1914 home's renovated bathroom. Inspiration struck when Lars, a designer with Oregon-based tile manufacturer Pratt & Larson, finished a marine-life tile collection. He realized its colors and patterns perfectly fit his own bath's remodeling project.

The room—small at just 7×8 feet—had last been updated in the 1940s. The couple ripped out the old fixtures and claimed 2 feet of width from a closet in an adjoining room. The bathtub moved from under the window to an adjoining wall. Lars separated the tub from the shower, accommodating the separate fixtures by

trimming the tub. While shorter than the standard 4 feet long, its 24-inch-depth and angled sides allow plenty of room for a good soak. A grab bar makes entry and exit a breeze. "It's very comfortable," Geoff says.

In front of both tub and shower, a tiled 10-inch-step runs the length of the room, making it easier to climb into the tub and marking a transition to the frameless glass shower door. On the opposite wall a half-wall separates the toilet from the vanity. Lars crafted storage cabinets to fit the revamped space. Bifold doors on the upper cabinets over both sink and toilet open away from the centered mirror.

By themselves the fixtures make fine use of the modest space, but it is the bath's tile artistry that turns the room on its head. Lars incorporated every one of the 25 styles of relief tiles from the marine-life collection, crafting a static aquarium full of murals and mini dioramas. Tiles arranged in the murals—three in the tub and two in the shower, including the diorama on the toiletry ledge—vary slightly, but are all double-banded with shaped nautical-inspired tiles. Two mural border tiles frame the mirror, while a sea of sculpted fish swims along the vanity's edge. Tone-on-tone relief tiles mark the bottom of the step and extend around the room as a baseboard. On the floor a beach of sand forms with limestone, inset with mini field tiles, while watery 4-inch field tiles in various glazes create changing waves on the walls.

Geoff, who works with paint, color, and design at a paint store, took one color from the field tiles, mixing it with a tiny amount of Japan color—highly concentrated pigment—in cobalt blue with paint thinner to coat the poplar cabinets. Geoff then wiped off most of the color, and sealed the surface with a low-sheen polyurethane. The color fits perfectly with the ocean handiwork. "The cabinets instantly gained some age and depth with the blue-over-green wash," Geoff says. "Now they look great next to the sea-life tiles."

DOORS OPEN OUT, AWAY FROM THE MIRROR. A HALF-WALL SEPARATES THE TOILET FROM THE SINK SURFACE. RANDOMLY DROPPED-IN RELIEF TILES INTE-GRATED INTO THE SURFACE OF THE WALL FIELD TILES PROVIDE GOOD RESTING PLACES FOR THE EYE.

A SCHOOL OF FISH SWIMS ALONG THE VANITY EDGE; SCULPTED SEA CREATURES FORM THE EDGE ON THE CUSTOM SINK. NEARLY EVERY SURFACE IN THE SMALL ROOM RECEIVED SOME SORT OF TILE TREATMENT.

MARINE SCENES FORM THE BACKSPLASH; AN ACRYLIC SHELF BELOW THE FRAMED MIRROR HOLDS BATH NECESSITIES.

SUAVE RESTYLE

Actress Jean Harlow would feel right at home in the update of the 1940s master bathroom in this Pasadena, California, showhouse—but so too would anyone bathing in this luxurious room's fabrics, finishes, and spa accessories.

Interior designer Jean Horn began by removing the dated fixtures and color scheme—mirrored vanity countertop, turquoise linoleum flooring, and floral wallpaper. Instead, she chose a neutral, adaptable palette with just a hint of color.

SCONCES PAIR WITH A NICKEL-PLATED SINK STAND, ADJUSTABLE MIRROR, AND ACCESSORIES. ALL COMPLEMENT THE COLOR SCHEME.

ANTIQUE SILVER LEAF ACCENTS THE DRAWER PULLS IN THE DRESSING AREA, WHILE OPEN SHELVES PROVIDE DISPLAY SPACE. THE SHAVING SINK HAS A HAMMERED NICKEL-PLATED FINISH.

THE ELEGANT LINES OF THE GOOSENECK FAUCET
CONTINUE THE LUXURY THEME.

TILES WITH JUST A HINT OF CELADON FORM THE TUB
SURROUND, BUT THE EYE TURNS UPWARD TO THE
ELEGANT MARBLE TILE MOSAIC IN A GREEK KEY PAT-
TERN. A HANDHELD WAND AND STATIONARY SHOWER
COMPLETE THE COMPOSITION.

"The goal was to take the existing footprint of the bath and update it, make it fresh and new," Horn says.

The updated space, divided into two distinct dressing areas and a shared bathing space, has a sophisticated timelessness that appeals to both men and women. Hints of celadon, white, and ivory appear throughout, starting with gray and taupe veins in the white polished marble floor and a hint of seafoam green tinting a marble dressing table top. In one vanity alcove, crystal-accented lamps and a curvy silk chair with antiqued silver-leaf legs add just a whisper of a feminine aura. For a touch of the masculine, in a second alcove a hammered finish appears on the nickel-plated shaving sink. Antiqued silver leaf covers the lip drawer pulls that extend from the cabinets, which were painted with a striated gray-green glaze. Throughout both dressing and bathing areas, assorted shapes of celadon marble tiles resemble wainscoting.

Details in the shared bathing area focus on a Greek key pattern, which gave the room a formal feel and reminded Horn of Roman baths. It's the cleverest of details, appearing in cloth tapes on the ivory window shade over the sit-down vanity, along the shower curtain's edge, and in a stunning bath tile mosaic. "It [the mosaic] creates a focal point and adds interest and texture," Horn says.

The mosaic also frames the tall stationary showerhead and handheld wand. At the bathing area's sink, classic sconces cast light on an adjustable mirror, shiny polished-nickel faucets, and a nickel-plated sink stand. "They become sculptural elements in themselves," Horn says of the new plumbing fixtures.

The range of light colors provides just enough contrast, while every detail complements the plush palette. Even the cool-silver accessories, from the frames that hold wall prints to the toothbrush holders, help the room avoid any sense of the neutral blahs. It is, as Horn intended, glamour without glitz.

Condo Conversion

Though Rosemary and Paul Gauthier loved their condominium retreat in the California desert, the bathroom had worn out its welcome. "It was claustrophobic," Rosemary says, recalling how a wall that separated the toilet and sink crowded the entire space. Compounding their disaffection, old patterned wallpaper left the space feeling dated and visually busy.

"It was very 1970s," says Rosemary, who prefers painted walls. "It just wasn't my style."

Realizing they needed more space but couldn't expand the room's dimensions, they removed the awkward divider wall. This allowed room to expand the vanity and re-create a space that is roomier for guests and more luxurious for the Gauthiers. "We wanted a remodeling emulating five-star hotels," Rosemary says.

Extended by 4 inches, the cabinet beneath the countertop now contains three generous dresser-size drawers.

The previously underused closet boasts custom-made cabinets, providing space for both the homeowners and guests. Three louvered doors on separate tracks allow easy access and replace unwieldy sliding doors. With space at a premium, cabinets that match the vanity allow the closet doors to remain open without making the space feel cluttered or disjointed.

Stone tile establishes a luxurious, natural-feeling

A CUSTOM-MADE BASIN FEATURES LIMESTONE TILE AND MOSAIC DETAILS. A BATHTUB SPOUT SIMPLY AND ELEGANTLY RISES OVER THE SINK'S WIDE BORDER.

TRAVERTINE PROVIDES AN AGELESS AND COMFORTING TEXTURE IN THE SHOWER, ON THE FLOOR, AND ALONG THE COUNTER EDGE.

Mosaic-stone sink basin

Custom-made closet cabinets

Tub faucet on the sink

foundation. Replacing the original tub and shower combination, the new open shower stall features a travertine surround. The same material forms a woven, herringbone pattern on the floor and creates an extended edge on the vanity. Using small limestone tiles, the woven pattern delicately repeats on the vanity countertop.

The sink basin, discovered while searching for stone tile, provides the final decisive element. The custom-crafted basin features limestone with mosaic tile and pebble accents. While the charm is evident, the plumbing needs are not. Since a standard sink faucet could barely reach the expansive stone basin, Paul creatively installed a tub spout instead. The large, curving fixture now adds a smooth, polished element to the rough stone environment.

For the Gauthiers, a small space did not mean compromising luxury. A stone foundation, a touch of handcrafted character, and a little creative plumbing transformed their bath to suit their needs and to serve their guests.

"We did not need a larger place," Rosemary says, "just one more luxurious that would work to our lifestyle."

MAXIMIZING SPACE AND MATCHING THE VANITY, THE CUSTOM-MADE CLOSET CABINETS PROVIDE NEEDED STORAGE AND MAINTAIN A CLEAN, UNCLUTTERED APPEARANCE. LOUVERED DOORS ON SEPARATE TRACKS ARE EASY TO OPEN AND SHUT, AND ARE SLICKLY UNOBTRUSIVE WHEN EITHER OPEN OR CLOSED.

DECORATIVE ELEMENTS, SUCH AS CANDLES AND A SPRAY OF FLOWERS, HAVE A COUNTERTOP HOME THANKS TO A SINK POSITIONED AT THE FAR LEFT OF THE VANITY.

AN EXTENDED VANITY CREATES A SPACIOUS COUNTERTOP AND PERMITS BROAD, DRESSER-SIZE DRAWERS FOR STORAGE UNDERNEATH.

9 POWDER ROOMS

Though petite in size, these rooms pack design power. Because powder room space is small and enclosed, experiment with bold colors or styles that you might hesitate to try in a larger, open room. Create a focal point for the room—a hand-forged basin, unique wall treatment, or piece of art— rather than giving equal visual weight to the entire space. Carve out enough storage space to stow basic necessities. A recessed niche near the sink can contain soothing hand lotion and a fresh bar of soap; a small drawer stows convenience items for visitors. Look for top-quality fixtures and materials: A powder room may be one of the most frequently visited rooms in your home.

ESSENTIAL ELEMENTS

In a small, constrained space the simplest, most elemental choices may make the biggest impact. Using uncomplicated, clean design and embracing the basic materials of wood, stone, and water, this constricted powder room became a space of serene balance where nothing seems excessive and nothing is wasted.

This room's Zenlike revelation focuses on the white bronze artisan-crafted vessel basin. The bowl's earthy, honed simplicity was the foundation for spare, elegant, Asian-influenced design throughout the room. Warm-tone maple cabinets and an angled limestone countertop add comfortable organic textures while defining a clean, contemporary look. Extending the natural, Asian sensibility, grass cloth provides an unexpected, subtly textured wall covering.

Unadorned minimalism unites the room's amenities as well. Sleek, wall-mounted faucet fixtures offer efficiency and elegance without cluttering the space. Narrow frosted light fixtures provide warm illumination and a crisp, unornamented geometric presence. With simplicity as its inspiration, a custom-made maple cabinet seems to float beneath the counter, its clever, angular construction opening to plentiful storage.

Even in a small room a thoughtful reduction to the basic elements creates harmonious form and function. Simple, clear design and natural, earthy materials make this space seem perfectly formed and balanced.

An above-counter, white bronze vessel basin exemplifies the simple, naturally harmonious vision for this space.

Providing needed storage and a distinctly modern element, the sleek maple cabinet maintains an uncluttered space as it appears to float beneath the counter.

Despite the cramped conditions, this bath is serene, uncluttered, and balanced, featuring Asian influences with contemporary sensibility.

HANDMADE BRONZE VESSEL BASIN

CUSTOM-MADE CABINET

NATURAL-FEELING, GRASS-CLOTH WALLCOVERING

DESIGN ID

Lisabeth Hayes gave her interior design skills a workout in a Chicago condominium bathroom remodel for herself and her husband, Michael Stell. Her personal style is reflected in a mix of natural finishes, antiques, and contemporary fixtures. "I love timeless classics. I wanted to update the bath in a way that was going to have some staying power and not look dated in a few years," Lisabeth says.

Bold blue and green iridescent glass mosaic tiles shimmer on the tiny bathroom's walls and at junctions in the honed marble floor. "Because this is such a small space, I wanted the walls to reflect as much light as possible," she says.

The diamondlike effect plays off other shapes in the room—an oval floating medicine cabinet at the sink, and a rectangular mirrored cabinet above the dressing table. Mahogany, cherry, and bird's-eye maple—inlaid on the drawers of the vanity—infuse the room with warmth. The brown patina plays off the neutral tile tones. "It's rare and elegant, with a little wear. I fell in love with it immediately," Lisabeth says.

Brushed fixtures finish off the room, a textural, eclectic space that reflects the aesthetic of its inventive owner.

AN ANTIQUE VANITY DRESSES UP THE ROOM WHILE A PRETTY EMBROIDERED STOOL ADDS JUST A BIT OF A FEMININE TOUCH TO THE ECLECTIC SPACE.

A PEDESTAL SINK, FLOATING MEDICINE CABINET, AND BRUSHED FIXTURES COMPLEMENT THE SHIMMERING TILES. A BURST OF FLOWERS HAS AMPLE SPACE ON THE DEEP, BRIGHT WINDOWSILL.

BROWN TONES ADD WARMTH TO THE ROOM, SOFTLY LIT BY SCONCES FLANKING THE RECTANGULAR MIRRORED MEDICINE CABINET ABOVE THE VINTAGE VANITY.

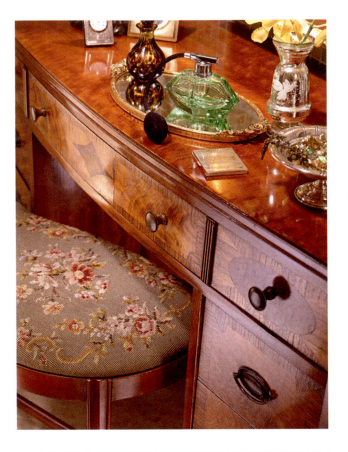

For designer Kelley Riddle, big challenges come in small rooms. "What I love about small spaces," she says, "is that you can design really neat, unusual things."

This cramped, windowless powder room offered just such an opportunity. Looking to produce a refreshing, spirited ambience, Riddle brought the outdoors inside. The tiny space resembles a garden gazebo, complete with flowers climbing trellises, and leaves underfoot. On a soft, ocher-glazed background a mural of pale flowers and muted green vines graces the walls. Framing slate tiles on the floor, handmade tile leaves form a wistful border.

With barely space to open the door, Riddle dismissed the idea of a cabinet and vanity combination, opting instead for a bronze wall-mounted faucet and a single ceramic bowl basin nestled in a twisting, branchlike stand. For storage a thin cabinet boasts a low-sheen, metal-bronze finish that resembles the faucets. Botanical prints and an antique mirror complete the transformation, turning a bland powder room into a charming homage to Victorian gardens.

"I break the rules a lot," Riddle admits, reflecting on her approach to the space. "Do something different. You're not in a powder room long enough to get tired of it."

AN ORGANIC-INSPIRED BASIN STAND AND AN ANTIQUE MIRROR SAVE SPACE WHILE CAPTURING THE RUSTIC TONE OF A VICTORIAN GARDEN.

FEATURING PALE FLOWERS CLIMBING A WOOD TRELLIS, A HAND-PAINTED MURAL EVOKES THE COMFORT AND CHARM OF A GARDEN GAZEBO.

HANDCRAFTED LEAF TILES DECORATING A BORDER ON THE FLOOR SET A WISTFUL, NATURAL TONE.

It's a tiny slice of a room—just 10×4 feet—but Mamie and Greg Case's powder room packs a wealth of design punch, courtesy of inventive wall and window treatments and clever accent coordination.

Interior designer Ellen Duffy started with the wallpaper, a tone-on-tone harlequin pattern of large diamonds that breaks up the walls and provides visual interest. "The larger-scale pattern offers an element of surprise in the small room," Duffy says.

A paint treatment by artist Kathy Gauthier, in a motif that echoes the wallpaper, spruces up the original built-in dressing table. Black dots accent smaller diamonds, while the wood countertop received a faux marble finish. Black appears again in the dual sconces flanking the ornate gold and black mirror.

Natural light floods in from the window wall above the built-in. Sheer curtains of loosely gathered dotted Swiss fabric dress up the frame and disguise the window's off-center placement. Three soft, plump knots at the top of the valance and a delicate trim at its bottom complement the dressy fringe on the table's upholstered stool and patterned area rug. Together the neutral palette received just enough dress-up details to make this little powder room sparkle.

A PEDESTAL SINK FREES UP FLOOR SPACE WHILE EFFECTIVELY HIDING PLUMBING. A FRINGED UPHOLSTERED BENCH AND SOFT VALANCE OFFSET THE PAINTED WALL AND DRESSER ACCENTS.

A FAUX MARBLE FINISH TRANSFORMED A WOOD COUNTERTOP. A LARGE WINDOW WALL (NOT SEEN) WORKS WONDERS TO OPEN AND ENLIVEN THE SPACE.

A TRIO OF KNOTS ADDS A DASH OF INTEREST TO THE WINDOW TREATMENT, SEWN FROM SOFT DOTTED FABRIC WITH A DELICATE TRIM.

10 KIDS' BATHS

Turn bathtime doldrums into delight with a design that charms children and grows with them through the years. These children's bathrooms mix fun and practicality. Splash an eye-catching paint color on the wall; it brightens the room and it's easy to change when you and your child are ready for a switch. Make sure your child's personality shines through. Adding a few handcrafted tiles to a field of plain ones personalizes the room. Include safety features that make your little one feel big: A step stool with rubber feet encourages handwashing. Choose easy-care materials for the space so your child enjoys bath time, and you won't stress about cleanup.

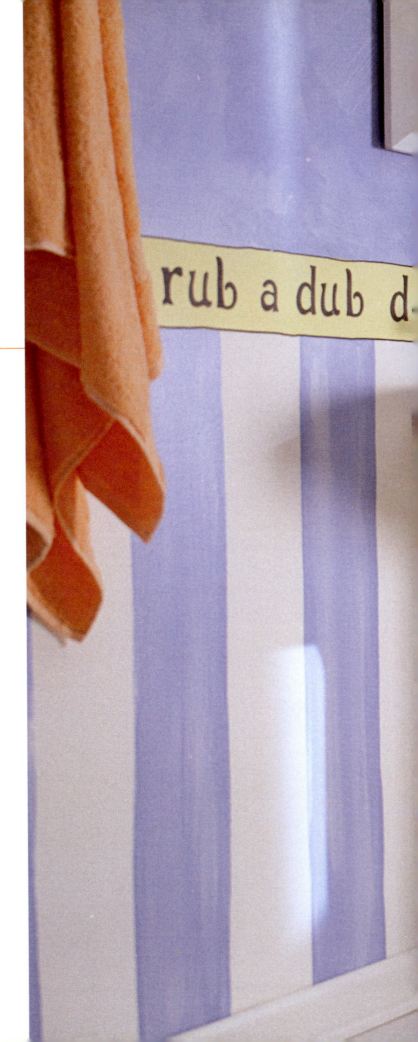

Everything Nice

Glowing with youthful exuberance, this bath reflects the verve and energy of growing girls. Blazing pink walls and vibrant gold countertop tiles are tempered only by the classic foundation of white cabinetry and floor tiles. With multicolored accent tiles on the floor and children's art framed on the backsplash, this design may seem firmly rooted in childhood, but it is ready for family adaptation.

Though the room is defined by the explosive joy of early youth, it matures with the occupants. The double vanity offers plenty of room to accommodate the varied transitions from dolls to braces. Large mirrors, spacious storage, and classic crossbar fixtures on the sinks anticipate maturing tastes and demands for personal space. A tub and shower combination addresses current bathtub fun while preparing for grown-up speed and convenience.

The powerful colors may define the moment, but the classic white floor and cabinetry permit an easy transition for changing tastes. In this sisterly bath, evolving decorative dispositions won't overwhelm the flexible functionality. A new coat of paint readily transforms the room's demeanor, accommodating all shades of sugar and spice.

Using bright tones and personalizing the space, this large vanity provides ample room for two growing kids and their changing needs.

Bold colors create a vibrant space, but the white floor and cabinets easily combine with any choice.

Tiny hands can easily manipulate Classic cross-handle fixtures. Their timeless style endures with maturing children.

A spacious, flexible vanity

Enduring, timeless fixtures

Classic white as a color foundation

MAKING WAVES

Jonathan and Pam Roleder wanted their son's bathroom to reflect his love of the ocean and the beach. But they didn't want to be left out to sea years later when tastes or circumstances might change. The problem inspired a pleasant compromise of beach-combing details and timeless tone.

To evoke the tidal theme, the walls' greenish blue shade of paint resembles seafoam. Covering the floor, shower wall, and vanity countertop, stone tiles feature a gritty, sandlike texture and a muted blue coloring.

Thoughtful details build the motif, but don't overwhelm the room's identity. A scalloped sink suggests a white clamshell left in the sand. Blue glass tiles featuring a swirling ocean wave design accent the shower and backsplash.

Although the bath was assembled with a boy's nautical interests in mind, the couple embraced a timeless look that would flow with changes. Neutral colors and delicate details are flexible enough to ride the currents of time. "We wanted a simple, classic look that wouldn't become dated or too juvenile as Max grew older," Pam says. "It's very simple and functional."

While future flexibility pleases the parents, for young Max the creative sea-and-sand combination means every day is a day at the beach.

SINCE THE BATH IS INTENDED FOR A CHILD, THE ROUGH FEATURES OF THE TILE COUNTERTOP ARE SMOOTHED AND DOUBLE THE NORMAL THICKNESS TO ELIMINATE SHARP EDGES AT THE OVERHANG.

WELL-SUITED FOR FUTURE ADULT USE, A SPACIOUS STEAM SHOWER FEATURES THE BEACH-INSPIRED TILE AND OCEAN BLUE GLASS ACCENTS. FOR A CHILD'S BATH THE ENCLOSURE SHOULD UTILIZE SAFETY GLASS.

INSETS OF A WAVEY PATTERN GLASS TILE ARE SPLASHED AROUND THE ROOM.

SUBDUED AND TIMELESS COLORS KEEP DECORATING OPTIONS FLEXIBLE IN THIS ROOM. NAUTICAL DETAILS AND A SAND-TONE TILE COUNTERTOP PROVIDE THE BEACH THEME'S FOUNDATION.

SCHOOLHOUSE ROCK

How do you mix schoolhouse aesthetic with the modern bathing needs of three children? Start with an old-style sink. It's just one element in the revitalized bathroom of Nancy Silverton and Mark Peel's circa-1910 home.

The bath's previous design—a renovation best characterized as "1970s white-tile excess"—was clearly out of step with the Craftsman character of the rest of the house. "It looked like a cheap motel bath," interior designer Lori Erenberg says.

Erenberg gutted the room, filling the lively retro-industrial space with found elements from old schools. "I wanted the room to look like an old-fashioned bathroom for kids, with some fun patterns and durable elements," Erenberg says. "The main idea was to put some character back into this room."

The space, a modest 7×11 feet, looks old-fashioned, but works like new. The trough sink came from an industrial supply catalog. With a deep bowl, in-between soap dish, and twin faucets, it's the perfect space-sharing spot for the couple's three children, Vanessa, Ben, and Oliver.

FUN PATTERNS MIXED IN BEIGE AND MUSTARD YELLOW PICK UP THE ROOM'S COLOR SCHEME WHILE ADDING KID-FRIENDLY COLOR.

A LONG CABINET, LEFT OVER FROM THE PREVIOUS DESIGN, WAS SAVED AND SPLIT IN TWO; THE SPACE BETWEEN HOLDS A MIRROR AND BENCH. THE COUNTERTOP ADDS MORE PREP SPACE, WHILE THE COLORS AND PATTERNS SUPPLY A RETRO SCHEME.

DEEP-TROUGH SINK FOR SHARING

SAVED CABINET SPLIT IN TWO FOR STORAGE

COMBO TUB/SHOWER FOR SPACE-SAVING

GLASS TUB ENCLOSURE TO BRIGHTEN THE ROOM

cabinet. She split it into two separate cabinets, adding a mirror and bench in the new in-between niche and tripling the counter space in the process. The cabinet doors and drawers repeat the mustard and beige colors from the rest of the room's finishes.

Once bland, the bath now is a warm and inviting room, with plenty of kid-practical finishes and Craftsman style. It's a long-term investment sure to last past the kids' growing-up years. "You don't want to put a lot of money into it when they're 5 and have them outgrow it when they're 8," Nancy says.

A RECESSED MEDICINE CABINET HOLDS BATH NECESSITIES. TILE APPLIED TO WAINSCOT HEIGHT IS PRACTICAL AND DURABLE. TWIN FAUCETS, SPLIT BY A SOAP DISH, DOUBLE THE SPACE FOR BRUSHING TEETH OR WASHING UP.

A FUN PAN-SHAPE SHOWERHEAD DIRECTS WATER OVER BATHERS. TILE PATTERNS IN THE SURROUND ADD A BIT OF COLOR KICK.

THE TROUGH SINK SERVES A DUAL PURPOSE. THE STYLE EVOKES AN OLD-SCHOOL CHARM AND THE DEEP BOWL HELPS MINIMIZE SPILLS. DESIGNER LORI ERENBERG FOUND THE SINK IN AN INDUSTRIAL-SUPPLY CATALOG.

Two sconces light a recessed, mirrored medicine cabinet framed in Craftsman style.

Tile in a mix of playful patterns and soft colors contribute the perfect decorative element for the room, from walls to floors to tub surround. Gray-blue tiles pave the walls to wainscot height; tiles in beige and a mustard yellow supply a bit of pattern and reappear in the tub surround. On the floor a retro hexagonal white and beige tile based on early 20th-century styles withstands the traffic from three sets of kids' feet.

Glass encloses the combination tub/shower, brightening the space. Smooth traffic lanes run between the sink on one wall, and toilet and tub on another. From the previous design Erenberg saved just a long built-in storage

Each day, Tammy and Jeff Koreman play their own version of cowboy, rustling together their three boys, Asher, age 7, and twins Elijah and Gabriel, age 5. What they didn't have in their home was a bathroom that efficiently herded the trio through their daily cleaning routine. By borrowing 4 feet from an adjacent bedroom and adding a lively Western theme, the couple turned the space into a no-fuss, no-muss workhorse.

The previous bath held just a tub, toilet, and small vanity. Bath designer Susan Chenault-Lawhorn split the new room into two halves. A pocket door separates tub and toilet from two sinks and a long vanity countertop, allowing privacy and sharing.

The boys' passions for cowboys and airplanes inspired the decidedly masculine—and practical—decor. The flooring that resembles pine actually is bath-practical ceramic tile. Dark cabinets with a worn look withstand wear and tear, as do solid-surface countertops. Each boy has his own set of drawers; a kid-friendly roll-out step allows them to use the spaces on their own until height catches up with them. A horseshoe tops dual medicine cabinets, and simple wooden pegs on a washed-blue rail hold towels.

Accessories allow the room's character to change easily as the boys get older. What won't change is the bathroom's ability to handle their daily stampede. "The idea was to have a space that would grow with the boys," Chenault-Lawhorn says.

A LEDGE ABOVE THE DUAL MEDICINE CABINETS ALLOWS FOR DISPLAY OF FAVORITE TOYS. A STAR MOUNTED ABOVE THE SINKS CONCEALS A NIGHT-LIGHT.

THE BOYS' HANDPRINTS SET ON TILES ARE A SWEET PERSONALIZED ACCENT. BUT THE SOLID-SURFACE COUNTERTOP STANDS UP TO LITTLE GROOMING NEEDS.

ROLL-OUT STEPS ACCOMMODATE HEIGHT ASSISTANCE UNTIL THE BOYS GROW TALLER. CERAMIC TILE HAS THE LOOK OF WORN PINE.

ROOM TO GROW

Jennifer and Don Stuart's five sons could field their own basketball team, but the boys needed a referee to negotiate the layout of their shared bathroom. The Stuarts remodeled the room in their Stevensville, Michigan, home for a more efficient, enjoyable setup that the boys—Drew, 18, Dack, 17, Owen, 8, Mason, 6, and Liam, 2—can use from toddler to teen.

The clever design eliminated a series of half-walls that separated a vanity from a toilet, sink, closet, and shower. The new long, open, and flexible rectangle has just enough room to move, and a dash of style too. A larger tub, fronted with a wood surround and flipped 90 degrees from the old tub's orientation, sits opposite a space-saving pocket door. Low horizontal windows above the tub minimize the sloped ceiling, while a long countertop and large mirror maximize grooming space around the two sinks. Across the room a tiled corner-entry shower sits next to a niche with a bench, hooks, and shelf, providing plenty of storage for towels, toys, and toiletry. Inside the door even more bath items reside within a tall storage cupboard.

In the fresh, fun space, traffic-absorbing materials such as white tile rising to wainscot height and a forest green countertop withstand the boys' daily wear and tear in the fresh, fun space. "Usually, we have more than one person in there at a time. It's easier to move around. It's so much more open, and it looks a lot better," Jennifer says.

A LARGE CLOCK ON THE FOREST GREEN VANITY COUNTER REMINDS THE BOYS OF THE TIME. PLENTY OF DRAWERS AND DOORS BELOW THE SINKS AND A TALL CABINET TO THE RIGHT OF THE SINKS FULFILL STORAGE NEEDS. A GRAY AND BLACK TILE BACKSPLASH SITS BELOW A LARGE MIRROR.

A CORNER ENTRY TO THE TILED SHOWER ALLOWS ROOM FOR A DRYING-OFF BENCH, TOWEL HOOKS, AND UPPER SHELF.

HORIZONTAL WINDOWS DRAW ATTENTION AWAY FROM THE SLOPED CEILING AND TOWARD THE TUB AND ITS WOOD SURROUND. DUAL SINKS PROVIDE PLENTY OF SPACE FOR THE FIVE BOYS TO SHARE.

WARM THOUGHTS

When Lynne and Steve Pearson decided to remodel the second-story bath shared by their two young daughters, they wanted a fairytale look perfect for little girls. "The old bathroom was very cold and gray," Steve says. So they enlisted the help of interior designer Lou Ann Bauer to create a bath that looked and felt warmer.

To avoid a complete remodel, Lynne and Steve asked Bauer to work within the original footprint of the space, staying true to the Arts and Crafts style of the home and keeping the fixtures in the same locations.

To accommodate the youngsters, they requested a doorless tub-shower combination with room to sit at one end of the tub surround. This makes it easier for Mom and Dad to help with bath time. Golden travertine floors warmed by radiant heat keep the bath cozy. A new buttery-hued vanity serves as the focal point, dressed up with fanciful cutouts in the fascia and glass-door upper cabinets for displaying toys and colorful towels. The white solid-surfacing countertop remains at a low 24-inch height to ensure that the children can easily reach the dual sinks.

Only now three children share the cheery bathroom. "We started out the project calling it the 'girls' bathroom,' so the bathroom has curlicues," Lynne says. "But then we had our son."

Now Lynne accessorizes with towels and other items in colors that appeal to all three children—at least until son Christopher eventually claims the third-floor guest bath as his own.

A MOSAIC-BRAIDED BORDER PUNCTUATES THE HEATED GOLD TRAVERTINE FLOOR.

GOLDEN HUES AND A LIGHTHEARTED MOTIF GREET THE PEARSONS' CHILDREN. A MULTICOLOR STRIATED ANTIQUE WASH GIVES THE VANITY ITS SUNNY HUE.

INDEX